GW01605786

THE HAPPY HOUSE CHILDREN

THE HAPPY HOUSE CHILDREN

THE HAPPY HOUSE CHILDREN

by

ENID BLYTON

COLLINS
LONDON AND GLASGOW

Reprinted in this edition 1976

© *Enid Blyton*

PRINTED AND MADE IN GREAT BRITAIN BY
WM. COLLINS SONS AND CO. LTD.
LONDON AND GLASGOW

THE HAPPY HOUSE CHILDREN

CONTENTS

CHAPTER ONE

Moving Day

JACK, Jane and Benjy were excited. They were going to a new house!

" This old one is so dark, and there are other houses all round it," said Jack. " We are going into the country now, Benjy, where we shall see more trees than houses, and plenty of grass everywhere, and wild flowers to pick, and cows in the fields."

" I don't like cows," said Benjy.

" You've never even *seen* a cow except in a picture!" said Jane. " So you don't know."

" I do know," said Benjy. " I don't like animals with horns. I shan't go into the fields if there are cows."

" You're a baby," said Jack. " You're only five, and you're still a baby. I'm nine and Jane's seven. We're big, but you're only a baby."

Benjy screwed up his face, and opened his mouth. He meant to howl as loudly as he could.

" Don't cry," said Jane, quickly. " Mummy said we weren't to quarrel, we were to be good. Soon the big van is coming to take all our things to the new house. You'll see it if you don't cry."

Benjy thought he wouldn't cry. He shut his mouth again, opened his eyes, and ran to the window. He gave a shout.

"The big van's here! Look! Oh, what a most enormous one! And here comes another one too!"

The big vans drew up to the house. Mummy opened the door, and the men let down the back of the first van.

"Now we shall see all our things being put on to the van," said Jane. "There goes the big table. And there goes Mummy's sewing machine. And there goes Daddy's armchair."

"Will they remember to take our toys?" said Benjy, suddenly. "I must have Monkey, I really must. I can't go to bed without Monkey."

"Well, put him under your arm now and then you'll be certain to have him, because Monkey will be with you," said Jane.

Benjy picked up old Monkey. He was a very old toy. He had first belonged to Jack, then to Jane and now to Benjy. So they all loved him and thought he was beautiful.

Monkey looked out of the window too. He had a long tail, a funny face, and loose paws that wagged about. All the grown-ups thought he was dreadful, but the children loved him and always took him away with them wherever they went.

" I shall carry Angela with me," said Jane, " then *she* will be safe too. She's my very best doll."

" And I'll take my aeroplane," said Jack. " I couldn't bear that to be left behind."

Mummy came into the nursery and smiled at them. " You must get yourselves ready now," she said. " Daddy is going to drive us in the car. We shall picnic on the way to our new house, and arrive there, we hope, at just about the same time as the vans do."

So they all packed into the car. There were the three children, Daddy, Mummy, and Hannah, their maid. It was a dreadful squash, and Monkey got sat on, but he didn't mind. Benjy sat on Hannah's knee, and Hannah sat on Monkey, though she didn't know it at first.

Off they went. All the children were excited. How lovely to go to a new house!

" What's our new house called?" asked Jane.

" I don't know," said Mummy. " I think it hasn't a name, only a number. But we will give it a name."

" Wait till we get there and see what it is like, then we'll name it," said Daddy.

They had a picnic by the roadside, and then on they went again and—at last they came to the little village where they were going to live.

It looked nice. There was a green in the middle of it. There was a pond by the green with white ducks swimming on it. " I shall feed them every day," said Benjy, pleased.

There were green fields everywhere, and hedges and trees. It was spring-time, so there were yellow primroses on the banks, and soon the bluebells would be out.

" I like this place, said Jane. " Look, is that a farm, Mummy? "

" Yes. We shall get our butter and our eggs and milk from there," said Mummy. " Look at the cows, Benjy! I do like those red and white ones."

" I don't," said Benjy. " They've got horns."

" Silly boy! " said Mummy. " Cows would look funny without horns. Look, there are sheep too. Soon they will have their thick woolly coats sheared off, and they will look queer and bare."

Big cart-horses went by with a clip-clop noise. They had shaggy hoofs and long whisking tails. The children liked them very much.

" I'm glad we've come to live here," said Jane. " Oh look—is that our house, Mummy? Oh, do say it's our house! It's the nicest one I ever saw! "

CHAPTER TWO

A Dear Little House

It *was* their new house! It was such a pretty one. It was white, with a roof made of thatch. It was long and low, and it had tall red chimneys. The front door was painted blue, and there was a lovely knocker on it.

"The knocker is a man's head!" cried Benjy. "It's a nice smiley head. I'll knock with it."

Knock-knock! The knocker made a very loud noise.

"It *is* a nice home, isn't it Mummy?" said Jane, as she and Mummy pushed open the little blue gate and walked up the primrose-lined path to the blue front door. "Fancy, we're going to live here!"

The children rushed into the empty house, running all over it, up the stairs and down. "Hannah, look at the cosy kitchen!" cried Jane. "Look, it's got a wide window-ledge for you to put your geranium plants on!"

Hannah was clever at growing geraniums. She had twelve plants, some red, some pink and one white. She always had them in the kitchen, and was pleased to see such a nice window-ledge she could put them on, in their new home.

"Where's my room?" cried Benjy. "I want to show Monkey where we are to sleep."

" Your room is a little one tucked up on the roof," said Mummy. " You and Jack are to share it. Go and find it."

Jane had a dear little bedroom too. It looked straight out on to two big cherry trees. She looked at them in delight.

" Mummy! I've got cherry trees outside my window, almost touching it. Oh, Mummy, won't it be lovely when they are out! I shall wake up in the morning and think there is snow outside, but it will be cherry blossom, smelling sweet."

" And in June you will be able to lean out of your window and pick ripe red cherries! " said Jack. " I wish *I* was having this room. Mummy, can't I have a room with cherry trees outside? "

" You've got an apple tree just below your window, if you look," said Mummy. " You will be able to pick apples! "

" This is a most lovely house," said Benjy, happily. " I like it. I like the garden. Come and see it, Jane and Jack."

The garden was certainly lovely. There were a lot of fruit trees in it, plenty of flowers, a big patch of grass, and, at the bottom a little stream!

" Oh! " squealed Jane. " A stream, Mummy! Is this stream ours ? Do say it is! "

" Well, I suppose the little bit that runs through our garden *is* ours! " said Mummy, smiling. " You will be able to sail your boats there."

" I wish we could keep a duck," said Jane. " Isn't it lovely to have our own stream, Jack? Aren't we going to have fun? "

"Here are the vans at last!" called Hannah from the kitchen door. "Now we can really set to work."

The children rushed to see the vans. The men let down the backs, and began carrying the furniture into the house.

Mummy stood in the hall telling the men where to put it. The children got in the way.

"Now, you go into the garden and play there by yourselves for a bit," said Mummy. "You will be a nuisance here. Go along."

The children went back again into the garden. A wall ran between their garden and the gardens next door. They wondered who lived there.

"We shall get to know lots more people," said Jane. "I hope they will be nice people, not cross ones, like old Mr. Topple who lived next door to our old house. He once shouted at me because I bumped into him round a corner."

Benjy and Jack felt sure that only nice people could live in such a nice village. They all felt very happy. The wind tossed Jane's curls about, and she held her face up to the breeze.

"Even the wind seems nicer here," she said. "Sort of friendly and playful."

After a while Hannah called to the children. "I've got your tea ready for you. Come along. You must be hungry."

They were very hungry. They raced in and to their delight saw that Hannah had laid their tea on the kitchen table, instead of in the dining-room.

"Oh, Hannah! Are we going to have tea in

your nice cosy little kitchen?" said Benjy. "Oh, Hannah, isn't it nice with the old table in it, and your four chairs, and your big rocking-chair, and the stool—and oh, you've all your geraniums on the window-ledge already!"

"Yes, and they're going to like being there," said Hannah. "The sun shines in there all day long. My, Benjy, look at your hands! Go and wash them at once. You don't suppose I'm going to have a dirty boy like that sitting down at my nice clean table, do you?"

They all went to wash, and then they sat down to tea. There was new brown bread and butter, jammy buns, and some chocolate cake. It was a very good tea.

"And milk left by the farm-boy!" said Hannah, pouring out their mugs of creamy milk. "Look at that!"

"Are the other rooms ready yet?" asked Benjy, getting all jammy. "Can we go and see them? Oh—where's Monkey? Where did I put him?"

"He can stay where he is till you've finished tea," said Hannah, firmly. "Any one would think you didn't like that old monkey at all the way you leave him about, Benjy."

"You left him looking at the stream," said Jack. "He's probably fallen in by now."

Benjy looked upset. "Now, don't you tease him," said Hannah. "You get on with your tea, and by the time you've finished, the vans will be gone, and you can go and have a look at the house, and see all the rooms full instead of empty."

The vans had gone by the time tea was over. Mummy put her head in at the door. " We've finished ! The house is almost straight—just the curtains to put up and the pictures, and the books to arrange. Come and see. "

The children rushed to look round. Benjy gave a squeal when he saw his bedroom and Jack's. It looked lovely. " I like the way the ceiling suddenly slants down at each side," he said. " Doesn't my bed look nice in the corner there? Are my toys in that cupboard, Mummy? "

" No, that's for your clothes," said Mummy. " Your toys are downstairs in the playroom. Did you know you were going to have a proper playroom of your own here? "

The playroom was lovely too. It was a small square room with a glass door that opened on to the garden. All round the side was a cupboard for toys, and all round the other side were shelves for books.

"You can arrange your toys and your books yourselves," said Mummy. "I've had them all put in the middle of the floor for you to sort out by yourselves. And as this is to be your own room, *you* will have to see it is kept tidy and nice."

"Oh, *yes*," said Jane, proudly. "Of course we will, Mummy."

"What are we going to call our nice new house?" said Daddy, coming in. "Any one got a good idea?"

"Cherry Trees," said Jane at once.

"Good idea, but there's another house in the lane with that name," said Daddy.

"We *must* think of a good name," said Benjy, frowning hard. "We simply must. It's such a nice *happy* house."

They all stared at the little boy, and then Mummy laughed.

"Benjy's right," she said. "It *is* a happy house and we hope it always will be. Let's call it Happy House."

So they did, and very soon the name was painted on the blue gate in big, bold letters. "HAPPY HOUSE." What a nice name for a dear little house!

CHAPTER THREE

Someone else for Happy House

VERY SOON the family was well settled in at Happy House. They loved it.

Jane loved her small bedroom that looked out on to the cherry trees. She watched the buds burst into snowy blossom, and lay in bed at night sniffing the sweet scent.

The two boys loved their room too, and Benjy said he was going to count every apple on the tree below the window. The straw thatch of the roof came right over Benjy's window, and the little boy watched a wren making a nest there.

The wren didn't mind Benjy. It didn't even mind Monkey either, when Benjy sat him up at the window to watch. It went on making a hole in the thatch, ready for its little wife to lay eggs in.

The playroom was fun. The children soon arranged all their toys there. The cupboard had three shelves in it, so Jack had the top one, Jane had the middle one, and Benjy had the lowest one. There were three bookshelves too, but the children had only enough books to fill two of them.

"We'll have some vases of flowers on the top shelf," said Jane. "They will look lovely against the pale wall."

“ And we can put our Noah’s Ark animals round the shelf too,” said Benjy. “ They don’t like being shut up in the ark. They told me so.”

So the Noah’s Ark animals were put on the shelf too, all in pairs. They looked grand. Mummy said it would be a nuisance to dust the shelf, if she had to move so many animals each day, but Jane said if Mummy would give her a duster, she would do it herself.

So, every day, Jane took the animals off the shelf, dusted it well, and put them back again. Sometimes Benjy put them back for her.

Jane picked flowers for the bowls and jars there too, and loved seeing them against the creamy walls of the playroom. There was a bright blue rug on the floor, and blue curtains at the window, so it really was a very nice playroom.

There was a doll’s house in one corner, and Jack’s fort in another. There was a bear on wheels that belonged to Benjy. He growled when you pulled a ring in his back. Benjy was still small enough to ride him.

“ I wish we had some geraniums, like Hannah’s, to put on *our* window-ledge,” said Jane. “ They would look so nice.”

“ I know what *I* wish,” said Jack, suddenly. “ I wish we could have a puppy! ”

“ You know we can’t,” said Jane. “ We’ve asked Mummy heaps and heaps of times, and she’s said no.”

“ Yes, but she only said no because we used to live in a big town, and Mummy doesn’t like dogs in a town," said Jack. "She might like dogs in the country. I'll ask her."

So he did. "Mummy, could we have a puppy?" he said. "We do so want one. Could we have one for our very own? We'll look after him so carefully."

"Well—I don't see why you shouldn't, now we've left the town," said Mummy. "But he must be *your* dog, children, and *you* must look after him! You will have to give him food, wash his dishes, see that he has fresh water, and teach him his manners."

"Oh, Mummy! Of course we will!" cried Jane and flung herself on her mother in delight. "Oh, a puppy of our own! What shall we call him?"

"Wait till we get him before you think of any names," said Mummy.

But they couldn't wait for that.

"I shall call him Scamp," said Benjy.

"No. That's an ordinary name," said Jack. "What about Trusty or something like that? Or Shadow. That's a good name for a dog. Most dogs follow their master as closely as a shadow."

"No," said Jane, "I shall call him Patter. Dog's paws always make a pattering noise when they run."

"That's a nice name," said Benjy. "I like that. We'll call him Patter. Pat for short, if we like."

"And Pitter-Patter for long," said Jack, with a laugh.

"Oh dear—I wish we could have him soon."

They hadn't very long to wait. One day they went to the farm to get the butter, and there they saw the little girl belonging to the farmer. She was seven, Jane's age, and she carried a very heavy armful of something.

" Whatever has she got ? " said Jack. He soon knew, and gave a yell. " Why, she's got a whole lot of puppies in her arms. Amanda, Amanda! Are those your puppies? "

Amanda stopped and smiled at them over the top of the four wriggling puppies. " Yes, they're all mine," she said.

" Aren't you lucky ? " said Benjy. "We want just one puppy, and you've got four! "

" Well," said Amanda, " I'll give you one if you like. They are English sheep-dog puppies—that's their mother over there!"

The children looked and saw Judy, the mother. She had a thick coat of grey hair, and masses of hair fell over her eyes, so that it looked as if she could hardly see.

" Oh. She's nice," said Jane. " Will the puppies be like her? Will their hair fall over their eyes like that? "

" Of course," said Amanda. "Well, which one do you want? They're all fat and cuddly and nice."

One wriggled out of her arms and ran to Benjy. It sat firmly down on the little boy's foot. Benjy was simply delighted.

" This is the one," he said. " This is ours. It came to me at once."

The puppy ran to Jane, making a pattering noise with its tiny feet.

" Patter! " cried Jane, and picked him up. " Pitter-Patter! Would you like to be our puppy?"

He licked Jane's nose and then licked Jack's cheek, as the boy bent over him.

" Pat! " said Jack in delight. " Oh, I do like you. Let me hold him, Jane. Oh, do let me have a turn at him."

So they each had a turn at holding the puppy, whilst Amanda stood with the other three.

" Amanda, I hope you don't mind us taking the very nicest of your puppies," said Jane, feeling rather guilty about it.

" Oh, *he* isn't the nicest," said Amanda, and held another one up. " This is the sweetest."

The others didn't think so. They thought their puppy was the very, very best. " Can we take him home now?" said Jack. "Had we better ask your mother first?"

"I'll ask her," said Amanda, and called out to her mother loudly. "Mummy! Can the children from the Happy House take one of the pups?"

"Yes, if their mother says so," called back Mrs. Busy.

"I'm *sure* Mummy will think this is exactly our puppy!" said Jane, joyfully. "Come on. We'll take him home and let Mummy see him."

So they ran home, Jane carrying the puppy carefully. He cuddled into her and seemed very happy.

Mummy was in the garden, weeding. Jane rushed at her, and held the puppy against her mother's cheek. The little thing at once licked her with its pink tongue.

"Oh!" said Mummy, surprised. "Jane, where did you get him? What a darling!"

"From the farm. He's ours, if you say so," said Jane. "Mummy, say so!"

"Of course you can have him," said Mummy. "What shall we call him?"

"Patter," said all three children at once. The puppy gave a tiny yelp. "There, he knows his name already!" said Jane. "Let's go and show him to Hannah."

And so it was that Patter came to Happy House, and pattered all over the house, even upstairs when he grew big enough. Everybody loved him and he loved everybody. But secretly Benjy was sure that Patter loved *him* most!

CHAPTER FOUR

Benjy is Very Upset

THE CHILDREN all had their own special jobs to do. Jane had to make her bed and the boys' beds too. She had to dust the two rooms well, and wind the clocks in each room.

Jack had to go any errand his mother wanted, and it was his duty twice a week to go to the farm and fetch the eggs and the butter.

Benjy had to fetch all the waste-paper baskets in the house after breakfast each morning and empty them for Hannah. This was a job he liked doing. There was never anything really exciting in the baskets, but Benjy always hoped there might be.

Once he found a tiny doll in Jane's basket. He looked at it and liked it. "Fancy Jane throwing that dear little doll away!" he thought. "I won't put it into the dustbin. I'll keep it myself, and let it live with my toys on my shelf. Monkey might like it for company."

So he put it beside Monkey in the playroom. Jane saw it there. "Oh, you bad boy!" she cried to Benjy, "you've taken my darling little doll! You're not to take my toys."

She snatched the tiny doll away, and knocked Monkey over. "Oh, you've hurt him!" said Benjy. "And I *didn't* take your doll, Jane. You put it in the waste-paper basket. You know you did."

"I did *not*!" said Jane angrily. "As if I would put one of my dolls in the waste-paper basket."

"Well, you did," said Benjy. "You're a naughty storyteller!"

"*You* are, you mean!" said Jane. "You're a bad boy. You took my doll and you told a story about it!"

Benjy began to cry. "Cry-baby!" said Jane. Benjy cried more loudly. Mummy came in to see if he had hurt himself.

"He took my little doll, and he told a naughty story about it," said Jane. "He said I put it into the waste-paper basket."

"Well, she did, she did," sobbed Benjy.

"Darling, I don't think Jane would ever put any of her dolls into the basket," said Mummy.

Benjy ran out of the room, crying as if his heart would break. To think that even Mummy didn't believe him! He went to the stream, and crouched over it. His tears fell into the water and made little plops.

"I'm raining," said Benjy. "I'm raining into the stream. I'll rain some more."

But when he tried, he couldn't. His tears dried up, and he sat back. He felt very hurt and very angry. He *had* found that doll in the basket. Jane and Mummy should have believed him. He always told the truth.

He stayed out there by the stream all morning. He wouldn't come when anybody called him. Nobody knew where he was.

Jane went upstairs with her waste-paper basket, and her little doll. She put the basket beside her little dressing-table, and sat the doll on the table, where she always sat. Then she dusted the room well, and went downstairs to play.

Mummy went up to Jane's room later on to see that she had done it properly. Mummy wouldn't let anything be done badly. If it was done badly it had to be done all over again.

She looked round the room. Yes, Jane had done it very well. Good little Jane! Mummy could always trust her to do her jobs well.

She was just going out of the room when she happened to look into the waste-paper basket. And to her great surprise, she saw the little doll lying at the bottom of it!

"Well!" said Mummy, "what a queer thing! Surely Jane *hasn't* put it in her waste-paper basket!"

She took out the doll and put it back on the dressing-table. Just at that moment the wind blew. The curtain billowed into the room, and knocked the little doll off the table. It fell into the basket below!

"There now!" said Mummy. "That's what must have happened before! The wind knocked the doll over. Benjy was telling the truth when he said he found Jane's doll in the basket! Poor little Benjy! I didn't believe him and Jane was so cross with him."

She went downstairs and told Jane what she had seen. Jane went very red. Oh dear—how she had scolded poor Benjy. Of course if he had found the doll in the basket, he must at once have thought it had been thrown away—so he had kept it for Monkey.

Jane rushed upstairs and got the doll. She rushed downstairs, almost knocking Patter over in her hurry. He ran at her heels in wonder. What was all the hurry about?

"Benjy!" yelled Jane. "BEN-JEE! I want you."

There was no answer. Benjy wasn't going to talk to anyone that morning. He wasn't going to go in and have any dinner. In fact, he didn't think he would ever in his life go indoors again, he had such a horrid family!

Mummy came out with a beautiful red ribbon fluttering from her fingers. She called Benjy too.

"Benjy! Benjy dear, I want you."

Still no Benjy came. Jane ran down the garden and saw Benjy crouching under a bush by the stream. He looked cross and miserable.

"Go away," he said. "I don't like you."

"Oh, Benjy, I've come to say I'm sorry I was so horrid!" cried Jane. "You were quite right, the doll was in the basket—but I didn't put her there. The wind blew the curtain and knocked her into the basket. That's what happened. I'm sorry, Benjy. Look, I've brought you the doll for yourself. You can have her."

Benjy smiled. "I feel better now you're sorry," he said. "I'd like the little doll. She was company for Monkey. You're nice, Jane."

Then Mummy came up with the red ribbon.

" See what I've found for Monkey," she said. " Come and put it round his neck, Benjy. He will look fine. I'm so sorry I thought you told a story. I know you always tell the truth."

" Yes, I do," said Benjy, beginning to feel much better. " Mummy, I rained on the water. My tears went plop just like the raindrops."

" Funny little boy! " said Mummy. " Come in and make Monkey look grand."

So in they went, Benjy all smiles. " It just shows, Mummy, that you mustn't call people horrid names till you're quite certain about things, doesn't it? " said Jane. " Benjy, you can have a very long turn of having Patter on your knee, next time we all nurse him."

" Oooh, I'd like that! " said Benjy. And he certainly did, especially when Patter licked his bare knees till they were quite wet !

CHAPTER FIVE

Oh, Where can Patter be?

ONE DAY the children took Patter for a walk. They often took him for walks, and he loved them. He could follow very well at their heels, and he always came when he was called.

"Don't go over the marshy fields," called Mummy, as they set off. "Keep on the dry ones. You haven't your rubber boots on."

Patter jumped round them as they went down the lane. Whenever any one of them said, "Heel, Patter!" he ran behind, and kept his nose so close to Benjy's heel, or to Jane's or Jack's that he bumped against them.

"He's really a very, very good dog," said Jane. "Oh, I say—look at those simply enormous buttercups over there! Let's go and pick a bunch."

They set off towards the big golden buttercups. But they hadn't gone very far before they found that the ground was very wet.

"It's marshy ground," said Jane. "Better go back. You know what Mummy said."

"It's not far to the buttercups," said Jack. "Look—let's jump from tuft to tuft of grass, and then we shall be all right."

So they began to jump—but suddenly Jane slipped and fell right down in the wet field. The

water squelched up, and Jane felt her frock being soaked through at the back. Her shoes and stockings were wet too. Jack pulled her up.

"Oh, dear!" said Jane. "Oh, dear, whatever will Mummy say? She said we weren't to go over the marshy fields."

"Let's go back," said Benjy, and he tried to step to the next tuft. But his feet too went into the watery grass, and his shoes were soaked.

It took them quite a long time to get back to dry ground. Jack was the only one not wet.

And then they found that Patter wasn't with them! He seemed to have disappeared completely.

"Gracious! Where's Patter?" said Jane.

"Patter! Patter! Pat!" shouted Jack. But no little puppy came.

" Whistle," said Jane. " I can't whistle properly, Jack, and Benjy can't whistle at all—so you must whistle and whistle."

Jack had a good whistle. He whistled for a long time, then all the children called and called, but still there was no Patter.

" He's lost," said Jane, almost in tears. " Oh, why did we try to cross that marshy ground? I expect Patter didn't want to get his feet wet, so he tried to get round another way, and got lost. Oh, he'll be so miserable and unhappy! "

The children hunted everywhere for Patter, but they couldn't find him. They were very sad. Benjy cried bitterly, for he loved Patter with all his heart.

" It's our fault he's gone! " he said. " We didn't take any notice of him when we were in that marshy field, and now he's gone."

They went home at last, very miserable. Mummy was in the garden, working. She looked surprised when she saw such sad faces.

" What ever is the matter? " she said.

" Oh, Mummy—we did what you said we weren't to do—we went into the marshy fields and got our feet wet—and we forgot all about Patter," said Jane. " He's lost. Mummy, shall we ever find him again ? "

" Poor Patter," said Jack. " We called and we whistled, Mummy, but he didn't come."

" I want Patter," said Benjy screwing up his face to howl.

Suddenly there was a high little bark and the

puppy rushed gaily round the corner of the house! He flung himself on the children, and they went down on their hands and knees and hugged him. He licked their faces over and over again.

"Patter! Where have you been?" they cried.

"He must have been much more obedient and more sensible than you," said Mummy. "He came straight home when he saw you floundering about in the wet fields! I wondered what had happened when I saw him scratching at the front gate."

"Oh, Patter, I *am* glad to see you," said Jane. "How *could* we have forgotten you, even for a moment?"

"Isn't he clever, to know the way home and come all by himself?" said Benjy. "Why, even *I* might get lost, and not know the way home from those fields."

"Well, I'm glad I've got a good dog even if I've got bad children!" said Mummy, and she laughed.

"Woof!" said Patter, proudly, just as if he understood, and he wagged his tail so fast that it could hardly be seen!

CHAPTER SIX

The Kitten and the Cuckoo-Clock

SOMETIMES the children climbed on to one of the walls that ran down the side of the garden, and looked into the one next door.

On one side lived Miss Plum, and Jack said she ought to have a P on the end of her name, and be called Miss Plump, because she was so round and plump and cosy-looking.

She really looked rather nice, but Mummy said she didn't like children, so they mustn't call to Miss Plum, or make too much noise on her side of the garden.

" Why don't some people like children? " said Jane, surprised.

" Well, you see, it's quite likely that the only children those people have known at all well, have been rude, noisy, rough children, with no manners at all," said Mummy. " And of course they don't like *those* boys and girls, and they think that all children must be like them. So they dislike them very much."

" Oh," said Benjy. " Do you suppose she would think we were horrid children too, then, Mummy? "

" She might! " said Mummy. " Anyway, don't bother Miss Plum please. Let her get used to you, and perhaps she will like you."

" Mummy, I do so wish she *would* like us," said

Jane, " because, you know, Miss Plum has got a cuckoo-clock, and I've never seen a cuckoo-clock in my life. Hannah says that when it's twelve o'clock, a little door opens at the top of the clock, and the cuckoo flies out, waves its wings, and calls cuckoo twelve times. Then the cuckoo goes back into the clock and the door shuts."

Benjy thought this sounded wonderful. He longed and longed to see the cuckoo in the clock. So did Jane, but Jack laughed. He said he was too old to bother about cuckoos in clocks.

Sometimes Jane and Benjy sat on the wall just when it was what they called " cuckoo-time " which meant something o'clock—two o'clock, or four o'clock or eleven o'clock perhaps—and they heard the cuckoo shouting, " Cuckoo, cuckoo, cuckoo! " inside Miss Plum's house.

" If only we could see it! " sighed Jane.

But they didn't dare to ask Miss Plum, of course. They slid down from the wall as soon as they saw her.

Then one day they saw that Miss Plum had a kitten in her garden! It was such a darling, quite black with four white paws and a white nose. It rushed about all over the place, and chased the bees, and patted every nodding flowerhead.

" I wish we could stroke that kitten," said Jane. " Oh, look, Benjy—I do believe it's going to the hole at the bottom of the wall. It may squeeze through! "

It did squeeze through! Then Patter saw it and came pattering up, surprised. He hadn't seen a kitten before. He sniffed at it, and the kitten patted him on the nose.

"Oh, isn't it lovely?" said Jane, and she picked it up. She called to Hannah. "Hannah, do look—the next-door kitten has come in!"

"Well, you'd better take it back," said Hannah. "They may miss the little thing."

"Could we have a little play with it first?" said Benjy.

Jane suddenly pulled him away up the garden in excitement. "Benjy! I've got a fine idea! I really have. Let's take the kitten back just about twelve o'clock—and maybe we shall hear and see that cuckoo-clock! We could go in at the garden door, and take the kitten to that room like we've got, with the glass door. That's the room the cuckoo-clock is in!"

"Oooh, yes," said Benjy. "That door's open to-day, and we could peep in and say: 'Excuse me, Miss Plum, but we've brought back your darling kitten.'"

"It's nearly twelve o'clock now," said Jane. "Quick, let's go. You don't feel afraid, do you, Benjy?"

"No. Not if I'm going with you," said Benjy.

They picked up the kitten, told Patter not to come, and went round to the garden gate next door. They went in and walked round to the back of the house, where the glass door swung open.

Miss Plum was sitting inside, writing. "Please," said Jane, "we've brought your kitten back, it's a darling one!"

Miss Plum looked up and said something, but Jane and Benjy didn't listen. They were staring in joy at the cuckoo-clock. It was simply lovely.

It was made of carved wood, and there was no glass over the face. Two big hands pointed to the figures. It was just twelve o'clock.

A door above the face blew open suddenly and the children jumped. A wooden bird flew out, with painted blue wings. It flapped them up and down, opened its beak, and the children heard: "Cuckoo! Cuckoo! Cuckoo!" twelve times!

Then the cuckoo shot back, the little door slammed, and there was silence.

"*Oh*!" said Jane, delighted. "How lovely! Miss Plum, aren't you lucky to have that clock to see every day?"

They suddenly remembered that Miss Plum didn't like children, and they said a hurried good-bye and ran home. But they couldn't forget that cuckoo-clock.

They told Jack about it. He was cross that they hadn't let him go too, although he had said he was too old to bother about cuckoo-clocks.

"I know how you can see it!" said Jane. "We can perhaps get the kitten through the hole in the wall again and then *you* can take it back, Jack. You can choose a time just before the cuckoo calls the hour."

So they tempted the kitten through the hole again, by dragging a bit of paper on a string. And just before three o'clock, Jack carried the tiny thing round to Miss Plum's.

And he saw and heard the cuckoo in the clock. He really thought it was the nicest clock he had ever seen. He rushed back home as soon as he had heard the cuckoo calling three o'clock.

Then, to Miss Plum's great surprise, the Happy House children began bringing back her kitten a dozen times a day, always just before the cuckoo flew out of the clock. She didn't know they came because of the clock. She began to think they must like coming to see *her*, and she was pleased.

"It's the first time children have ever seemed to like me enough to come and see me," she thought, and she was glad.

And then the children got a great surprise, for a little note came from Miss Plum, asking them all to go to tea with her the very next day!

CHAPTER SEVEN

Tea with Miss Plum

"MISS PLUM wants you to go to tea!" said Mummy, in surprise. "All three of you! Well—I thought she didn't like children."

The children didn't want to go. It was one thing to slip in with the kitten and hear the clock cuckooing, but it was quite another to go to tea, and have to talk politely, and be on their best behaviour with someone who didn't like children.

"Don't let us go, Mummy," said Benjy. "I can't behave well enough. I should spill my milk or something."

"Of course you can behave well enough," said Mummy. "As Miss Plum has been kind enough to ask you, you must go. If you don't like it, you can come back home at five o'clock. Miss Plum has asked you to be there at four."

"Mummy, don't make us go!" begged Jane. "Patter will be so lonely."

"Then he'll have to be lonely," said Mummy. "No, you must certainly go. Come in at half-past three, please, and get ready."

How the children grumbled to one another! How Benjy scowled! He told Monkey all about it in a loud voice when Mummy was about, but Mummy took no notice at all.

At four o'clock the three children were ready,

dressed in clean blouses, with clean faces and hands and knees. Patter was very sad when he found he was to be left at home.

To the children's disappointment they did not have tea in the cuckoo-clock room. Still, it was a lovely tea. The children felt shy at first and hardly spoke. Miss Plum felt shy too, and as she was not used to children she did not know what to say.

But the tea itself was very nice. There were cucumber sandwiches, which they were not allowed to have at home, and buns with strawberry jam on, and biscuits with little sweets on top, and a big jam roll, the biggest the children had ever seen.

" It's the sort of jam roll that says: ' Have two helpings of me! ' " said Benjy.

" No—it says: ' Have *three* helpings,' " said Miss Plum, and all the children stared at her in surprised delight. They began to think that Miss Plum was rather nice.

They remembered their manners very well and did not take anything till they were asked. They remembered to look after Miss Plum too, and offered her something when they saw her plate was empty.

" Could we just see the cuckoo come out at five o'clock before we go ? " said Jane, after tea.

" Have you got to go so soon ? " said Miss Plum. " Well, well—I suppose it's very dull for you to come to tea with me."

She looked rather sad. Jane didn't like people to look sad. " Well, you see," she said, " we know you don't like children, and we are trying to behave very

very well. But we're afraid if we stay longer than five we might not be able to go on behaving properly."

Miss Plum looked astonished. Then she suddenly laughed. "*I'm* trying to behave well, too," she said. "I'm very shy, you know, and I was afraid you might not like me, so I've been on my best behaviour too. Shall we all stop being quite so polite, and say what we want to say, and do what we want to do? What would you like to do?"

"I'd like to look at that man on the mantlepiece who's got a nodding head," said Benjy at once. "I should like to make his head go on nodding for a long long time."

"And I should like to play with your kitten," said Jane. "Where is she?"

"Well, I shut her up," said Miss Plum. "I thought you must be very tired of her, because you had to keep bringing her back here. I thought you must think her a very tiresome kitten."

"Oh, we *love* her!" said Jane. "Will you promise not to be cross if I tell you why we kept bringing her back?"

Miss Plum promised. So Jane told her how they longed to see the cuckoo come out of the clock, and how they had tempted the kitten through the hole in the wall, and then taken her back each time just before the cuckoo came out of the clock.

"Then we saw the cuckoo, you see," said Jane.

Miss Plum laughed again. She fetched the kitten, and she brought a strange puzzle for Jack to do. It was six bits of polished wood, and you had to fit them all together in a certain way to make a square. Jack loved it.

They watched the cuckoo fly out at five o'clock, flap its wings and call cuckoo five times. Then Miss Plum brought out some funny old snap cards, and they all played snap.

" I'm not very good at snap, I'm afraid," said Miss Plum. " I never was."

" I'm not either yet," said Benjy, feeling pleased. Most grown-ups were far too good at snap, he thought. But Miss Plum wasn't at all. In fact, she was out of the game and had lost all her cards even before Benjy.

The cuckoo flew out and called six o'clock. The children were surprised.

" Gracious! " said Jane. " Has a whole hour gone? Oh, dear—I suppose we ought to go home."

" Just stay and hear my musical box," said Miss Plum. "I had it when I was a little girl, and loved it. Perhaps you will love it too."

She brought out quite a large box. She opened it and the children saw that under a sheet of glass was a big brass cylinder with little points all round it. Miss Plum wound the musical box up, the cylinder began to go round, and music came from all the little brass points, as they caught on to little brass pegs when they turned.

" Oh, it's like tinkling fairy music! " said Jane, full of delight. " It's the loveliest thing I've ever heard! "

" Isn't Miss Plum lucky? " said Benjy. " She's got a cuckoo-clock, a kitten, a nodding man and a fairy musical box. Wind it up again, please, Miss Plum."

The time went by, and suddenly there came a knock at the front door. "Now who can that be?" said Miss Plum, surprised. She went to open it.

It was Mummy! "It's almost seven o'clock!" she said. "I wondered what had happened to the children. It's past Benjy's bed-time. I'm afraid they have stayed far too long, Miss Plum. I'm so sorry."

"Mummy, we've had a most wonderful time!" said Jane, her eyes shining. "Miss Plum has such lovely things. Have we really got to go? Can Miss Plum come to tea and see Patter?"

"I've loved having them all," said Miss Plum, her eyes shining as brightly as Jane's. "I've never known such friendly, well-behaved children. I'm so glad you've all come to live next door."

Mummy was delighted to hear this. She felt proud of the three children then. She smiled and took Benjy's hand.

"Well, I'm sure the children are glad *you* live next door!" she said. "Please come to tea one day this week. But don't ever let the children bother you too much."

"They can come and see me whenever they like," said Miss Plum, in a nice warm voice. "It will be lovely to have three new friends. Benjy, would you like to take the nodding man home for one night?"

"Oh, *yes*," said Benjy. "Can I put him on the table by my bed? Then I can nod his head for him first thing in the morning. And Miss Plum—would you like me to lend you Monkey for the night? You can have him if you like."

Now Benjy had never in his life lent Monkey to anyone, and Jane and Jack stared at him in surprise. He had gone rather red, because he didn't really want to lend Monkey. But Miss Plum had been so very kind.

" Oh, no thank you," said Miss Plum at once. She knew all about Monkey because Benjy had told her. " The kitten might nibble him, you know."

" All right," said Benjy, very glad to think Monkey would be with him that night after all. " Well, good-bye, and thank you for a nice time."

" Aren't we lucky? " said Jane, in her bath that night. " We've got a very nice new friend."

" Miss Plum is luckier still! " said Mummy, drying her quickly. " She's got *three* nice new friends! "

CHAPTER EIGHT

Patter has an Adventure

ONE DAY Mummy told Jane she could go and feed the ducks that swam in the pond on the village green. Jack and Benjy had gone out with Hannah and Jane felt lonely.

" I'll take Patter," said Jane. " He'll like to see the ducks."

So the two of them set off, Jane carrying a paper bag with some bits of bread in it. She came to the pond and called to the ducks. They came swimming up, lovely white birds with yellow beaks.

Jane fed them. Some of them turned themselves upside down so that just a tuft of tail showed above the water. Patter couldn't make out why they did that. He barked every time.

When Jane had fed the ducks, she went to the old wooden seat under the chestnut tree by the bus-stop and sat down to wait for the bus to come. It was fun to see the people getting off the bus and into it. It was fun to say " Good morning " to old Mrs. Potts back from the market, and to watch the conductor helping everyone on most politely.

The bus came up the lane by the green with a big rumbling noise. It stopped by the seat, and Jane got up to see all the people getting off and on. Patter was most excited because there was another dog. This dog got on the bus with its master. Just

as the bus was going Patter made a flying leap at it, and got on to the conductor's little platform!

Jane gave a squeal. "Patter! Patter, jump off! Oh, Patter, quick, you'll be carried away!"

Patter went inside the bus to find the other dog. Jane stood still, watching the bus go down the lane. Then she ran after it. She must catch it! She must make it stop so that she could get Patter!

The bus went faster than she did. It went round the corner, and on to the next stop. Jane knew it stopped there quite a time, because it was a busy place. If only she could get there before the bus went on again!

Jane ran fast, panting hard. She *must* get Patter, she must, she must! Why, someone might steal him! He might never get home again. The bus went on and on for miles!

She turned three corners, and then the next bus-stop could be seen. But alas—no bus was there! It had gone. Jane hadn't been able to run fast enough.

She walked up to the seat and sat down. Tears rolled down her cheeks, because she felt so tired and hot and sad. Now Patter would never come back.

"I can't walk back all that way myself," she thought. "I wonder if I've got any money in my pocket. If I have I could catch the next bus back and tell Mummy what has happened."

But she hadn't a penny in her pocket! An old man sitting on the bus-stop seat saw her wiping her eyes and spoke to her. "Haven't you anything for the bus? Here is a threepenny bit."

"Oh, thank you," said Jane. "If you'll tell me your name and address I will pay you back when I get my pocket money."

"I never let anyone pay me back," said the old man. "It's so nice to be able to help."

Jane thought he must be a very nice kind of man. She put the coin safely in her pocket and waited for the bus to come that would take her back home. She thought of poor Patter travelling miles and miles away from her in the other bus, and a tear fell down her cheek again.

The bus came at last. Jane got into it and sat down. The conductor came and she gave him her fare. Then she sat and jerked about as the bus went off. Her feet didn't quite reach the floor, and her bare legs swung to and fro.

Suddenly she felt something wet against them. She looked down. Nothing was there. Then she felt something warm and wet again—like a tongue!

She slipped off the seat and looked under it. And there was Patter! He was frightened, and was lying down, his eyes wide and scared. He had been most astonished to smell Jane's legs in front of him, and had given them a few loving licks. But he hadn't dared to come out from under the seat.

"Oh, *Patter*!" cried Jane, joyfully. "You bad little dog! I ran miles after you. How did you get on *this* bus?"

The conductor came up when he heard Jane speaking. "Oh, he's your dog, is he?" he said. "Well he jumped on my mate's bus at the Green, and when he found that nobody owned him, my mate didn't know what to do. He thought he had better put him on another bus, going the opposite way, and have him put off at the Green again, hoping he'd go home. So when his bus met mine, we both stopped, and he handed the little dog over to me."

"Well, he's mine, he's Patter," said Jane, picking him up and hugging him. "He jumped on a bus all by himself! What can he have been thinking of! Patter, you must never, never do that again!"

Jane and Patter got off by the duck-pond and they both ran home. What an adventure to tell the others!

Patter stopped to talk to the short-legged Scottie dog who lived in the village. " Woof! " he said. " I've been for a ride on the bus! "

" Come on, Patter! " cried Jane. " Don't boast! I want to get you safely home before you have any more adventures! "

But Patter had to stop and tell the big collie dog about his great ride, and the little brown and white puppy he sometimes played with. He even tried to tell a big black cat sitting on the wall, but the cat shut her eyes and took no notice at all.

" Patter! Come along at once! " said Jane. " *I* want to tell your adventures, too! Do come on. We'll tell Mummy and Hannah and Jack and Benjy. They'll hardly believe it! "

So Patter trotted back to Happy House at Jane's heels. When they got there Mummy called out to Jane. " Where *have* you been, darling? I was getting quite worried about you! "

Then Jane told everyone about Patter's bus-ride and he stood by proudly, wagging his tail. Benjy felt sure he knew why Patter had jumped on the bus. " He wanted to be a bus conductor, like me! " said Benjy. " Didn't you, Patter? "

" Woof," said Patter, and Benjy said that meant, " Yes, of course! "

CHAPTER NINE

Benjy goes to Bed

ONE DAY Benjy had a cold. He tried not to sniff, and he tried not to sneeze. But he couldn't help coughing, and Mummy heard him.

"Benjy, you have a cold," she said. "You had better go to bed. Let me feel your hand. Yes, it is far too hot. Go upstairs, dear, and I will come in a minute and tuck you up."

"Mummy, I *can't* go to bed to-day. You know we're all going to tea with Auntie Mary," said Benjy. "I won't give my cold to anyone, I really won't. I'll keep it all to myself."

"You will be really ill if you go about with a cold like that," said Mummy. "Off you go upstairs, Benjy. It looks to me as if you'll be in bed for two or three days."

Benjy opened his mouth and howled. He didn't feel well, but he didn't want to go to bed, he couldn't bear to miss going out to tea, and felt very miserable indeed.

But he went upstairs. He began to undress himself, sniffling all the time, feeling very sorry for himself.

Mummy came up and helped him into bed. "Mummy, don't go to Auntie Mary's to-day," begged Benjy. "Don't leave me all by myself."

" Hannah will be in, dear," said Mummy. " The others will be disappointed if I don't take them. You mustn't be selfish."

" But I don't *want* you to go! " wailed Benjy, miserably. " You're not to go. I won't let you go."

Mummy didn't take any notice. Benjy turned his face into the pillow and made it all wet. Mummy put Monkey beside him, and a little jar of boiled sweets and a glass of lemonade.

" Now you try and go to sleep," she said. " Then you will soon be better."

Benjy hoped and hoped Mummy and the others wouldn't go off to Auntie Mary's that afternoon. He didn't want them to go without him. He thought of the nice chocolate cake Auntie always had, but somehow he didn't feel very hungry when he thought of it. He sneezed and coughed. Poor Benjy—he certainly had a very bad cold.

" Good-bye, darling," said Mummy, at half-past three, popping her head in to see if he was awake. " We are just going to catch the bus. We shall be back soon. Hannah will bring you some tea."

Benjy heard the front door slam. He felt lonely and miserable. He cuddled Monkey. He thought everyone was horrid, and he told Monkey so.

" Did you hear that slam? " he asked Monkey. "Well, that was the front door, Monkey. All my family have gone out to have a good time, and they've left me alone in bed."

Monkey stared at him kindly. Benjy cuddled him again. " I hope I shan't give you my cold, Monkey. I won't breathe over you. I'm glad you're not horrid, too. *You* wouldn't leave me in bed and go out to tea, would you?"

At four o'clock Hannah came up with a tray. Two pieces of bread and butter and jam, and two biscuits and a bit of cake. There was a glass of milk too.

"I don't want anything," said Benjy, pushing away the tray and nearly upsetting the milk. "I'm cross, and sneezy and lonely. You come up here and sit with me, Hannah."

"I can't dearie, I'm busy making jam to-day," said Hannah. "You wouldn't want it to burn, so that it was all wasted, would you?"

"I wouldn't care if it did," said Benjy, beginning to feel that nobody loved him and nobody wanted him. "Everything's horrid. Nobody loves me at all."

He pushed away the tray again and this time some of the milk slopped over on to the cloth.

"There now!" said Hannah. "What a mess you've made!"

"I'm glad I've made a mess," said Benjy. "Now you'll have to stay and clear it up. Stay with me, Hannah, please do."

"You let Monkey drink up that milk you've spilt," said Hannah, and she picked Monkey up and put his nose into the little puddle of milk. Benjy was cross. He snatched Monkey away.

"You've made his face wet! Now he'll get a cold, too. Where's my hanky to wipe him with? Poor Monkey—there, I've wiped your nose for you."

"You're a little crosspatch," said Hannah. "You

eat some tea like a good boy, and you'll feel better. Let Monkey have some of the biscuit. You always say he likes biscuits."

"Well, he doesn't like them to-day," said Benjy. "Neither do I. I don't want any tea. I'm feeling very ill indeed, Hannah. I don't believe I'll ever be able to get up again in my life."

"Well, what a silly boy!" said Hannah. "Shall I stay with you just five minutes then?"

"No," said Benjy, going into a sulk. "Go away. I don't want you or anybody now. I feel as if I'm going to be in a very bad temper for the rest of my life."

"Well, I'll go then," said Hannah. "Listen—there's the front-door bell Now, whoever can that be?"

Very soon Benjy's door opened and in came Miss Plum! "Hallo, Benjy!" she said, "I met Mummy in the road and she told me you were in bed all alone. I'm all alone to-day too, so I wondered if I could come to tea with you."

"Oh, *yes*," said Benjy, sitting up. "Nobody else wants me at all, so perhaps I would do for you, if you're lonely."

"This looks a nice tea, but there's not very much of it," said Miss Plum, looking at the tray. "I've made some ice-cream to-day. Shall I go and fetch some? Do you feel like any?"

"Well, that's just exactly what I *do* feel as if I could eat!" said Benjy. "Could you go and get it? I do hope, Miss Plum, that you won't catch my cold."

" Oh, no. I never catch colds," said Miss Plum. " I'll go and get the ice-cream now. You start on the bread and butter and milk."

Benjy started. Miss Plum soon came back and dear me, what a big bit of ice-cream she had brought for Benjy! He was so pleased. She had brought something else too! She had with her the big musical box and the man with the nodding head!

" I thought I'd lend you these till you are better," said Miss Plum. " Mummy and Hannah are too busy to sit with you long, I know, and Jane and Jack mustn't come in, in case they catch your cold. So perhaps these things will stop you feeling lonely."

" Oh, they *will*! " said Benjy, in delight. " Oh, Miss Plum, I shall really *love* having a cold if I can play the musical box and watch it all the time, and nod the little man's head. I shall try and make him nod his head in time to the music! "

They had a lovely time. Benjy ate his ice-cream very slowly to make it last a long long time. He played the musical box all the time, and wound it up himself. He tapped the little nodding man to make him nod quickly.

" Look at him! " said Benjy. " He goes nid-nod, nid-nod, nid-nod, exactly in time to the tune. Miss Plum, isn't he clever? "

" He's a dear little man," said Miss Plum. "I'm very fond of him. I had him when I was a little girl and I can't tell you how many times he has nodded his head at me."

" He likes nodding his head," said Benjy. " Isn't it nice to have someone who never shakes his head and says no to you, Miss Plum? Now I'm going to wind up the musical box again. You tell me the tunes it plays."

Monkey sat and listened to the tunes. The nodding man nodded brightly and cheerfully all the time. Benjy looked at his empty plate of ice-cream.

" It's rude to lick round it, I know," he said. " But I would so like to. It was such a very nice ice-cream."

" It isn't rude to lick the plate when you're ill," said Miss Plum. " Monkey could have a lick, too. I'll bring you in some more to-morrow, if you like."

Benjy licked the plate, and then Monkey got *his* nose ice-creamy, too. " Now we'll have a game of snap, shall we? " said Benjy, feeling very much better. " You play snap nicely, Miss Plum. You don't call ' Snap ' too quickly."

So they played snap until it was time for Miss Plum to go.

When Mummy and Jane and Jack came home Mummy ran upstairs to see how Benjy was. He was looking ever so much better, and the musical box was playing loudly.

" I've had a lovely time," said Benjy. " Miss Plum came to tea with me, but she's gone now. She's lent me her musical box and nodding man till I'm better. I've had a nicer time than if I'd gone with you to Auntie Mary's."

" We had chocolate cake again! " called Jane from outside the door.

" Well, I've had ice-cream! " said Benjy.

" I've brought you back a book from Auntie Mary," said Mummy. " And Jane, Jack and I have each brought you a tiny motor-car for your toy garage. There you are! "

" Oh! " said Benjy, in delight. " A red one, a blue one and a green one. *Thank* you, Mummy. I'm sorry I was so cross. I thought nobody loved me, and now I see that everybody does! I was silly, wasn't I? "

" You were rather," said Mummy, kissing the top of his head. " It must be nice to have a cold, Benjy, if you get as many treats as this! "

" It is," said Benjy. " Mummy, I shall never mind having a cold again, because Miss Plum is always going to lend me her musical box and her nodding man if I do. So that would make a cold very nice to have, wouldn't it? "

" You will have to lend Miss Plum something if ever she gets a cold! " shouted Jack, from outside the door.

" Yes I will! " shouted back Benjy. " Only she says she never does. Isn't it a pity? I could have lent her Monkey."

CHAPTER TEN

Jane and Mummy's Birthday

"IT's Mummy's birthday next week," said Jane. " I've got five shillings saved up. I shall go out to-day and see what I can buy with it."

So out she went—but soon she came back in tears. She had lost her little purse with the five shillings in it.

" I've looked everywhere, simply everywhere," said poor Jane. " Someone must have picked it up. It had my name and address inside. They ought to bring it back."

But nobody brought it back, and Jane was sad about it. " I wouldn't have thought there were such mean people in the world! " she said. " If *I* found somebody's purse *and* money, *and* their address inside, I would take it back that very minute. Mummy, why are some people so horrid?"

" Well, I expect they were not taught these things when they were children," Mummy said. " It is only those boys and girls who learn the right things when they are little that grow up into good men and women. That is why I like to teach you so many things."

Jane didn't know what to do about Mummy's birthday. She would only have one sixpence before it came. She couldn't possibly ask Mummy for money to buy a present, because that would seem as if Mummy had brought her own present, instead of Jane. So she told Hannah and asked her what she could do.

"Well, now," said Hannah, "this is a very busy time of year for me. I'd be glad of a little help from you, Jane, and what's more, I'll pay you for it. I want to make red currant jelly, and I want the ripest red currants in the garden, and I want them taken off their stalks."

"Oh, I could easily do that!" said Jane. "Do you want some to-day?"

Hannah did, so Jane went out and picked a big basket full. It took her a long time.

Then she went and sat down at the kitchen table and began to pull them off the stalks. "Don't do them with your fingers," said Hannah. "Take a fork and you can get them all off at one stroke then."

Jane didn't stop till she had finished the job. Hannah was very pleased with her. She gave her a shilling.

"Oh, thank you!" said Jane, pleased. "Now if only I can get three shillings more, I can buy Mummy a little red vase I saw in the village shop. I know she would love it."

Hannah must have told Miss Plum that Jane wanted jobs to do, because next time Jane went out into the garden, Miss Plum looked over the wall.

"Jane!" said Miss Plum. "Can you write nicely?"

"Well, I can if I try hard," said Jane. "I can write in ink, you know."

"I wonder if you'd like to copy out one or two notes for me," said Miss Plum. "I have to send out a notice about a Sale of Work, and I'm rather too busy to write them all out myself. I'd be very glad to pay you threepence a note if you'd do them."

"Oh, *yes!*" said Jane, joyfully. "I'm badly wanting money for Mummy's birthday present, Miss Plum. I'll come over now, if you like. I'll do my very best writing."

The notice wasn't very long. It was this. "A Sale of Work will be held at the Church Hall on Monday, July 21. Please come."

Jane was rather a slow writer, and it took her ten minutes to copy out each note nicely. If she made a mistake she began again. She was too honest to let Miss Plum pay her for a badly-written notice.

She did six by tea-time, and Miss Plum was very pleased. She gave her one and sixpence and Jane put the money happily in her pocket.

The next few days Jane earned two shillings. She weeded a garden bed for Daddy and earned a shilling. She washed all Mummy's flower-vases very carefully and earned sixpence. She got a three-penny bit from Hannah for stirring some raspberry jam to keep it from burning.

Then she got threepence from Miss Plum for taking the notices of the Sale of Work round to a good many people.

She had her Saturday sixpence too, so she had five shillings to spend on Mummy's birthday. She bought the little red vase, and she bought a red comb in a case for a shilling. She was very pleased.

Benjy had bought a shoe-horn because Mummy had broken hers. Jack had spent ten shillings! He had bought a dainty brooch with a tiny star in the middle of it. Mummy thought it was really beautiful. Daddy gave her a new pair of shoes, and Hannah gave her a new purse for her bag.

"How lucky I am!" said Mummy, as she got ready for her birthday tea. "I shall wear new shoes and get them on easily with my shoe-horn. I shall comb my hair with my new comb. I shall wear my lovely new brooch, and have on the table a dear little red vase full of flowers. And in my bag I shall have a new purse for my money."

Miss Plum came to tea, too. Benjy ran to her.

" Miss Plum, have you brought Mummy a birthday present? It's her birthday to-day, you know."

" Well, I *have* brought her one," said Miss Plum. " But I'm not at all sure if she'll like it."

" Show it to me first," said Benjy. " I shall know at once if she will like it."

So Miss Plum showed him what she had brought. She had a pretty blue and silver box in her hand, tied up with silver ribbon. Benjy untied the ribbon, took off the lid and looked inside.

" Oh! " he said, " it's a box of little chocolate animals. Oh, look at this horse—and this giraffe—and here's a little lamb. Oh, Miss Plum, I am sure Mummy will like this present. I simply love it myself! "

" Well, I thought if Mummy didn't like it very much you could all share it," said Miss Plum, and she gave it to Mummy.

Mummy loved it, and everyone had an animal by their plates at tea-time. Benjy said he couldn't possibly eat his chocolate horse because it was too beautiful. But he did, of course.

They all had Mummy's birthday cake, the one that Hannah had made. It was such a lovely one.

" You must all wish," said Mummy. " A birthday cake has a bit of magic in it, and wishes may come true if you wish whilst you are eating the first piece."

So they all wished, Miss Plum too, but nobody told their wishes, because if they did they wouldn't come true. Even Patter had a piece of the cake, and

Benjy was sure he wished whilst he gobbled it, because he looked so solemn.

"Well, good-bye," said Miss Plum, when Mummy's tea-party was over. "Good-bye, little Happy House family. I'm so glad I know you. Good-bye!"

"Come again!" said everyone. "Everybody is welcome at Happy House! So come again."

"Wuff!" said Patter, going to the gate with Miss Plum. "What a nice family I belong to! And what a lucky dog I am!"

THE END

THE HAPPY HOUSE CHILDREN AGAIN

CONTENTS

CHAPTER ONE

Happy House Again

You will remember that Jack, Jane and Benjy lived in a white house with a thatched roof, and a blue front door. It was called Happy House, because it really was a happy house with happy people.

There was Jack, who was nine, and quite a big boy.

There was Jane, who was seven. She had curly hair, and was a great help to Mummy.

There was Benjy, the smallest. He was five. And there was Patter, the sheep-dog puppy, who loved everybody in the house.

There were Mummy and Daddy, and there was Hannah the maid, who kept pots of red and pink and white geraniums on her window-sill.

Next door lived Miss Plum, a round, plump, cosy-looking person, who hadn't liked children at all till she had met Jack, Jane and Benjy. But she liked *them* very much. They liked her too, and they liked her cuckoo-clock, her kitten and her musical box as well.

It was summer-time. The sun shone down very hotly, and the sky was a blue as the cornflowers in Miss Plum's garden. Patter tried to find a cool place to lie down in but he couldn't.

" It's August," said Daddy. " We always go to the seaside in August, but I thought we wouldn't this year, because I have had to spend a lot of money on Happy House. But if you think so, Mummy, we'll go, as it is so very hot."

"*Oh no!*" cried Jane and Benjy. "We can't leave Happy House the very first summer, Daddy!"

"We can paddle every day in the stream if we want to," said Jack. "That's nearly as good as the sea."

"Well, I agree with the children," said Mummy. "I don't want to leave Happy House this year. We'll go to the seaside *next* year."

The children went to tell Miss Plum. They hoped she wasn't going to the seaside either, because they would miss her so.

She was in her garden, in a little tent she had put up. It was striped red and white, and was open in the front to the breeze.

"Oh, you've got a tent!" said Jack. "I'd like a tent too—a wigwam, like the Red Indians have."

"Well, you could come and play Red Indians in *my* tent, when I go out if you like," said Miss Plum, putting her knitting down. "I know you won't spoil the tent."

"No. Of course we wouldn't," said Jack. "Oh, thanks, Miss Plum. We came to tell you that we're not going away to the seaside this year, and we hope you're not either, because we should miss you."

"Well, I'm not," said Miss Plum. "I've had a letter from my sister, who lives by the sea. I was going to go and stay with her, but she hasn't been well, so she can't have me."

Miss Plum took up a letter beside her on the garden table. She put on her glasses. " My sister asks me if I will have Tommy and Betty here to stay for a week," she said. " They are my nephew and niece."

" Oh," said Benjy. " Do you like them? "

" Well, you know, I never did like children till you came to live next door to me," said Miss Plum. " I'm afraid I didn't like Tommy or Betty. But perhaps now I know you three children so well, I shall like Tommy and Betty better."

" They can play with us," said Jack, thinking it would be fun to have two more children to play with.

" How old are they? " asked Jane.

" Tommy is eight, and he's a big boy for eight, I remember," said Miss Plum. " And Betty is seven, just your age, Jane."

" Oh well—it will be nice to have them to play with," said Jack.

" I hope you won't leave me out," said Benjy, looking solemn. " You'll all be older than me. I can't help being small."

" We won't leave you out, if you're big and don't cry," said Jack. " You cried again yesterday when you fell down and hurt your knee."

" I saw you had a bandage on," said Miss Plum. " Poor Benjy!"

" Oh, *I* don't mind! " said Benjy, looking brave. " I didn't cry much, anyway."

" You did. You howled," said Jane. Benjy went red and turned away. He was cross.

" Oh, so *that* was the noise I heard! " said Miss Plum. " I thought it must be Patter howling for his dinner, and I was surprised to hear what a wonderful yell he had! "

Everybody laughed, even Benjy. " Patter doesn't howl for his dinner," said Benjy. " He whines. He's so hot to-day, Miss Plum, that he pants all the time as if he's been running."

" And his mouth is too hot to keep his tongue in," said Jane. " So he hangs it out all the time. We all thought it looked very rude at first but now we've got used to it."

" When are Tommy and Betty coming? " asked Jack. " Won't they love the kitten—and your cuckoo-clock—and your musical box! "

" I hope so," said Miss Plum, and she looked rather doubtful. " I'll let you know when they arrive. I *do* hope they behave themselves."

CHAPTER TWO

Meeting the Bus

MISS PLUM called over the wall to the children three days later. "Jack! Jane! Benjy! I suppose you wouldn't like to go to the bus-stop and meet Tommy and Betty to-day, would you?"

"Oh *yes*," said the three children. "What time are they coming?" asked Jane.

"By the eleven o'clock bus," said Miss Plum. "I've their beds to make, and I would be so glad if you would go and meet them."

Mummy said they could. So, at a quarter to eleven they set off with Patter to the bus-stop. They sat down on the seat and waited. Soon the bus came round the corner and stopped.

Before anyone could get off the bus a boy pushed through the people and jumped down. He was about as big as Jack, but fatter. Then the other people got down, and last of all a little girl with a heavy bag.

"Oh, come on, Betty! You're always last!" said the boy.

"That must be Tommy—and Betty," said Jane. She and Jack and Benjy went to meet them.

"We've come to meet you," said Jane. "Miss Plum, your aunt, asked us to. We live next door."

"And we hope you'll be able to play with us," said Jack.

" Oh, are you Jack, Jane and Benjy? " said the little girl, pleased. " Auntie Sally told us about you."

" Come on, let's go," said Tommy. " You show us the way, Jack."

" Aren't you going to carry your sister's bag? " said Jane, surprised to see Betty dragging the bag by herself.

" Of course not! Betty likes doing things like that for me," said Tommy. " Don't you, Betty? "

" Yes," said Betty. But Jack didn't like to see Betty carrying the bag and he took it from her.

" My Daddy says that boys should look after girls, and carry things for them, and help them," said Benjy.

" Pooh! Girls are silly. Let them wait on *us*, that's what *I* say!" said Tommy, and he walked along with his head in the air, looking as if he owned the whole street.

Jack said nothing, but he carried the bag all the way.

" Did you come by yourselves this morning? " asked Jane. " Was it a very long journey? "

" Only about an hour," said Tommy. " That's nothing. I go everywhere by myself. I go out on my bicycle too, and ride for miles."

" Oh—have you got a bicycle? " asked Benjy. " Can you really ride it? Jack can't ride and he's nine."

" I can drive a car too," said Tommy. The others stared at him in astonishment.

" But no one's allowed to till they're sixteen at

least," said Jane. "It might even be eighteen. And you're only eight."

"Well, I know how to," boasted Tommy. "I've watched my father heaps of times, and one day when he leaves me in it alone I'm going to start it up and drive it down the street! I can ride a horse too."

"Gracious!" said Benjy, thinking what a wonderful boy Tommy was. "Jack and Jane want to ride, but we can't afford it yet."

"Once I stopped a runaway horse," went on Tommy. "I leapt at his head, hung on to the reins, and dragged the horse to a standstill. The people all cheered me, I can tell you!"

The others gaped at him. What a remarkable boy! Jack wished he could say he could do a few things too, but he couldn't think of anything.

"You take a turn at carrying this bag," he said, suddenly. "It's heavy."

"Betty will take it if it's too heavy for you," said Tommy. That made Jack go red. He wouldn't let Betty take it, of course. Daddy would never let Mummy carry anything heavy if he could help it.

"How's old Plummy?" said Tommy. It sounded rude to hear Miss Plum spoken of like that, but it also sounded funny. The children giggled and Tommy was pleased.

"She's a funny old thing, isn't she?" went on Tommy. "Full of 'don'ts' and 'mustn'ts.' Very boring to stay with."

The Happy House children were fond of Miss Plum, and loyal to her. "She never says 'don't' or 'mustn't' to *us*," said Jane.

" She's not a bit boring," said Jack. " I wish she was *my* aunt."

" She's very, very nice," said Benjy. " I like Plummy."

" Oh, Benjy—don't call her that! " said Jane quite shocked. " Suppose she heard you? "

" Well, I think Plummy is a nice name for her," said Benjy. " She *is* like a plum, a nice ripe, juicy sweet plum. We once thought she ought to be called Miss Plump, because she *is* plump, but I think Plummy's a much better name."

" Here we are," said Jack, opening Miss Plum's gate for Tommy and Betty. " Take the bag now, Tommy. See you later."

" Thanks," said Tommy, and took the bag. " Here, Betty, take it whilst I knock at the door."

" BLIM-BLAM-BLAM! " You should have heard the way Tommy banged on the knocker.

" How *dare* he knock like that! " said Benjy. " Plummy won't like it at all!"

CHAPTER THREE

A Game of Red Indians

IT RAINED for the rest of that day and the children did not see any more of Tommy or Betty. But the next day was fine, and they went into the garden.

Tommy was sitting on the top of the wall. "Hallo!" he said. "Come on over and play. We'll play Red Indians and have Plummy's tent for a wigwam."

"Oh, I thought of that too, the other day," said Jack. "Is Miss Plum in?"

"No, she's out," said Tommy. "So it's a good chance to make a noise. She's always saying 'Don't shout!' or 'Shut the door quietly' or something like that. Come along, all of you."

So over the wall they went. Jack and Jane each had Red Indian feather hats, and Benjy had a little band with ordinary feathers stuck into it.

"I'll have your hat," said Tommy to Jane and took it off her head. "Here, you give yours to Betty, Benjy."

"I don't want to," said Benjy. "I don't want to be the only boy without a feather hat."

"Look here, I'm Red-Eagle, the mighty chief," said Tommy, in such an awful voice that Benjy felt quite afraid. "You and Jane are the enemies. I've got to capture you and tie you up. Then I'll run off with Jane. This is my wigwam here."

He pulled Jack and Betty into the tent.

"You're my squaw," he said to Betty. "You will stay here and cook my dinner. Jack, you go out and stalk the enemy. Lie flat on your tummy."

He put his head out of the tent. "Benjy and Jane, run away and hide somewhere. Go on!"

It really wasn't a very nice game of Red Indians, because Tommy had all the fun. He ordered Jack and Betty about, he pounced on Jane and Benjy, and he dragged them to a tree near the tent.

"Tie that brave up!" he ordered Jack, and pointed to Benjy, who didn't look a brave at all, because he was quite afraid.

Jack tied him up. "Now take that squaw to my tent and guard her," commanded Tommy. "She's mine. I'm going to shoot Benjy and then scalp him."

He danced round the tree, yelling so fiercely that Benjy was scared. Then, to the little boy's horror Red-Eagle took up a bow he had made from a stick and a piece of string. He fitted a wooden arrow into it and took aim at Benjy.

"No, no! You're not to shoot at me!" yelled Benjy. "Jane! He's shooting at me! Save me!"

Jane rushed out of the tent. "You're not to frighten him!" she said fiercely to Tommy.

"How *dare* you talk to me like that?" shouted Red-Eagle. "You're only a squaw and you've been captured. Play the game properly or I'll tie you up and shoot you too!"

"Woof!" suddenly said a voice and Patter, the puppy, galloped into the garden. He had been out

with Hannah, the maid, but now he was back, longing to join in a game.

"Patter, save me, save me!" shouted Benjy, trying to wriggle free. Red-Eagle gave a wild yell that startled Patter almost out of his skin. He ran to Tommy and growled

"Call your dog off!" cried Tommy. "I'll shoot him if you don't!"

Then everything became muddled. Benjy broke the string that tied him and rushed to get the bow from Tommy. Jane flew to Patter. Jack fell over Jane and Betty began to howl.

In the middle of it all Tommy let loose the arrow and it hit Patter on the back. He yelped.

Then all the Happy House children turned on

him at once. " You hit Patter! You're cruel! "

" Give me that bow! "

" Oh, Patter, are you hurt? "

Then Mummy's voice came in great astonishment over the wall. " Children! What *is* the matter? Why are you making this dreadful noise? "

Nobody said anything. Jack, Jane and Benjy didn't want to tell tales. Patter barked loudly.

" I'm sorry we've been so noisy," said Tommy, at last. " It's the little ones—and the dog. He made himself a bit of a nuisance. Benjy and Betty are too little to play a game like this. We'll play something quieter."

Mummy went in. Tommy turned with scorn on the others. " Spoiling everything! " he said. " Making such a fuss. And those babies Betty and Benjy howling like that! Silly little cowards! "

Just at that moment Miss Plum came into the garden. She had been out, and had only just come in. She hadn't heard any of the noise at all. She smiled at them all.

" What good children! " she said. " Come along in and drink the ginger-beer I've got for you. Have you had a nice game, Tommy? "

" Lovely," said Tommy. " We're getting on fine, Auntie. The others made me their Red Indian chief, and we had some grand fun. Oh, look—there's the kitten. Couldn't we pretend she's a fox or something and hunt her? "

" No," said Jane, Jack and Benjy all together, glaring at Tommy over their ginger-beer. And for once Tommy said no more!

CHAPTER FOUR

Tommy Tells a Bad Story

THE CHILDREN didn't like Tommy. They didn't like Betty very much either. They thought she was deceitful.

" She broke one of the wheels off my tiny motor-car," said Benjy. " And she said she didn't."

" And she told Miss Plum that she saw me taking some of the raspberries out of the garden, and I never, never did," said Jane.

" Well, Miss Plum didn't believe her," said Jack. " She knows you wouldn't do a thing like that."

Tommy had plenty of ideas for games but he always wanted his own way and he always wanted to be chief in everything. His voice was loud, he was strong, and he liked ordering people about.

" He's done so many things, and he's so bold and brave," said Jane. " I wish *you* had done a few things he hasn't done, Jack. He seems to think we're such babies."

" Perhaps we are," said Jack, gloomily. " I've never been in a train alone yet, and he has, heaps of times."

That afternoon the Happy House children didn't play with Tommy and Betty. Mummy said it was time they played quietly by themselves in their own garden for a change. She wanted a rest.

They could hear Tommy and Betty playing next door. It was a game called Burglars and Policemen, Tommy, of course, was the policeman, and Betty was the burglar.

It wasn't a very quiet game. Jack wondered if he had better climb up on the wall and ask Tommy not to yell so much, because his mother was having a rest. But he felt that probably that would make Tommy shout even more loudly.

Just then there came a crash of glass. It was a very loud noise indeed. It came from Miss Plum's garden. Jack, Jane and Benjy stood still and listened.

They heard nothing after the crash, nothing at all. Not a whisper, not a footstep. What *could* have happened?

Jack sprang up on to the wall. He looked over and saw that the frame in which Miss Plum grew her cucumbers was broken. Three of the panes of glass were smashed in.

No one was in the garden at all. How queer, because Tommy and Betty had been there a few moments before! "I'll jump over and see what's happened to break the glass," said Jack, and he jumped down and went to the frame. A large stone lay in the frame.

Then he heard Miss Plum's voice. "Oh, Jack dear, what has happened? Surely you haven't broken my cucumber frame?"

A voice came out of one of the upstairs windows in Miss Plum's house. It was Tommy's.

"He threw a stone over the wall, Auntie. I saw

him from here. Betty and I were reading quietly up here and the noise did make us jump."

"Oh, Jack!" said Miss Plum, looking vexed. "I suppose it was an accident—but how careless of you!"

"I didn't do it, Miss Plum," said Jack. "I just jumped over to see what had happened."

"He's a bad storyteller!" came Betty's voice. "I saw him break the glass!"

Miss Plum said no more. She just went indoors, looking sad and vexed. Jack felt very upset. He looked up at the window but Tommy and Betty were not there any longer. He climbed back over the wall.

Jane was almost in tears, and Benjy looked alarmed. He couldn't believe that anyone could tell such a story. Jane put her arm round Jack.

"You didn't do it," she said. "How *can* Tommy be so bad? *He* must have done it? We didn't see him, it's true, but he and Betty were there just before the crash. They must have tip-toed off to the house at once."

The three children really didn't know what to do. If they went to tell their mother she would hardly believe that Tommy and Betty could tell such stories. And yet it was horrid to think that Miss Plum thought Jack had broken her frame.

"The only thing to do is to go and see Tommy and Betty after tea, and ask them to own up," said Jack. "We've always been taught to own up. Surely they will too, when we tell them what we think of them."

Miss Plum went out after tea. Jane saw her go and went to tell Jack. "We could go and see Tommy and Betty now," she said. "All of us."

So they went in. The side-door was open. Just as they got inside the rain began to fall.

"There's going to be a storm or something," said Jane, looking up at the black sky. "How lovely! I do love storms. I hope there's some lightning."

Tommy and Betty were upstairs in Tommy's room. They didn't seem very pleased to see the three children.

"Look here," said Jack, "you've got to tell your aunt it wasn't me. You know I didn't break that frame. It was you."

"Who told you to come here?" asked Tommy, in a fierce voice. "I'll tell Miss Plum you came in without being asked. I'll tell her you took some of her sweets!"

"You're a bad, wicked boy," said Benjy, suddenly quite shocked.

Tommy turned on Benjy, caught hold of him and shook him hard. "Don't you say things like that to me!" he said. "Do you know what I shall do, if you do? I shall get that Monkey of yours and drown him in the stream. See?"

Monkey was the toy that Benjy loved the best. He yelled when he thought of him drowning in the stream. Tommy was pleased. "And I shall take Angela, Jane's best doll, and break her in two!" he said.

The three children stared at him in despair. How

could you make a boy like that own up and do what he ought to do? He wasn't afraid of anything or anyone. He just did what he liked.

The rain struck hard against the window. Then a brilliant flash of lightning came, and lighted up the room, which had gone quite dark.

After that there came a crash of thunder. Jack, Jane and Benjy forgot about the quarrel and ran to the window. They loved a grand storm. Mummy had often let them get out of bed at night and watch one with her.

"What marvellous lightning!" said Jack. "Now—listen for the thunder!"

"Crrrrrrrrash! Rrrrrrumble-rrrroll!" went the thunder like guns not very far off.

Benjy turned round to tell Betty to come and see. But there seemed to be no one in the room. Where had Betty and Tommy gone?

Then he saw something funny sticking out from under the bed and he stared at it. It was somebody's foot!

"Look, Jane! Look, Jack!" cried Benjy. "Tommy's gone under the bed! Oh, he's afraid of the storm! Oh, what a baby he is to be afraid of the thunder and lightning. *I'm* not, and I'm only five!"

CHAPTER FIVE

The Thunderstorm

JACK and Jane stared in surprise. Yes, it was quite true, Tommy was hiding under the bed, and so was Betty. Well, well, well!

The thunder crashed again. A squeal came from Betty and a moan from Tommy. "Come out, sillies!" cried Jane. "Come out and see the lightning. It's lovely. Don't be such babies!"

Jack pulled out Tommy and Betty, giggling.

What! Was this brave Red-Eagle, the Red Indian chief? Was this the head of all the policemen? Was this the boy who ordered everyone about, and boasted of all he could do?

"Don't go, don't go," begged Tommy, clinging to Jack. "Stay here till the storm is over. Don't leave us."

"Well, we came here to ask you to be decent and own up," said Jack. "And you won't, so it's no good our staying. We'll go."

Tommy burst into tears. He clung to Jack and Jane as if he would never let them go. The lightning flashed again and he moaned.

"You can't leave me, you can't. I'm scared of storms. So's poor Betty. Don't go!"

Betty was sobbing too. She cuddled up to Benjy. "You stay here," she begged. "We're frightened."

"I thought you weren't afraid of anything, Tommy," said Jack.

"Yes, he is. He's afraid of storms and cows and snakes!" wept Betty. "And he's afraid of earwigs too."

"Earwigs!" said Jack. "Fancy being afraid of little insects like that! What a baby he is!"

"He's crying much worse than I ever cry," said Benjy. "Look at him. I hope the lightning and thunder come worse than ever. Jack, don't you think this storm is a punishment for Tommy because he told such a dreadful story about you?"

"I shouldn't be surprised," said Jack, trying to shake himself free from Tommy's hands. "Anyway, we'll go and leave him to his punishment. Mummy will be wondering where we are."

"No, no—*don't* leave me!" wept Tommy. "I'll tell Auntie the truth. I'll tell her it was me and not you. I will, I will."

"Well, I can hear her coming in now," said Jane. "I'll call her."

She went to the top of the stairs and called. "Miss Plum! Is that you? We're up here."

"Oh, are you? Poor children, I hope you are not frightened!" called back Miss Plum. "I'm just coming." She came in, surprised to see Betty and Tommy in tears.

"They're afraid," said Benjy. "Why are they afraid, Miss Plum? We're not afraid."

"Auntie, don't go out and leave us again!" sobbed Betty. "Another storm might come."

"Tommy's got something to tell you, Miss Plum," said Jack. "Go on, Tommy. Quick!"

Another roll of thunder came and Tommy trembled. He really was a baby! "Oh Auntie, it wasn't Jack that broke your frame—it was me," he stammered, his cheeks still wet with tears.

His aunt looked at him, and it was not a nice look. "How disgusting of you to put the blame on to someone else," she said. "I'm sorry I asked the children next door to play with you now. I won't ask them again, though perhaps, they might be good for you—but instead I'm now afraid you'll be bad for them, and I wouldn't have them spoilt for anything."

Tommy sobbed loudly. He was so ashamed of himself that he hardly knew where to look.

"You had better go straight to bed, both of you," said Miss Plum, in a stern voice that the children had never heard before. "I may perhaps send you home to-morrow. I'm not quite sure. I don't feel as if I want you to stay with me any longer."

Jack, Jane and Benjy thought they had better go. "Goodbye, Miss Plum," they said, in rather small voices.

"Good-bye, dears," said Miss Plum, and went downstairs with them. "I shan't send Tommy and Betty home to-morrow," she said in a low voice. "But I shall send them in to you to say they're sorry, and you can decide whether or not you want to play together any more."

CHAPTER SIX

Much Nicer Children

THE NEXT morning two miserable-looking children came round the garden-way to Happy House to find Jack and Benjy. Tommy hung his head and could hardly look the others in the face.

"We've come to tell you we're sorry," he said. "Oh, Jack, how can you like thunderstorms like that? And even little Benjy! I think you're the bravest children I ever knew!"

"No, we're not," said Jack. "Mummy says it all depends on how you're brought up. We asked her. She says if you see grown-ups being scared of anything, you get scared too. But if you see they don't mind a bit, well, you don't mind either. It's not being brave."

"But I do think you and Betty were babies," put in Benjy.

"Yes. You always boast so much of all the things you can do!" said Jane. "You make yourselves out to be so fine and grand and clever and brave—but all the time you are too frightened even of owning up to something you've done."

"That's much, much worse than being afraid of a thunderstorm," said Jack. "We wouldn't mind a bit being friends with children who were afraid of things—but we don't want to be friends with people who don't tell the truth or are too cowardly to own up to anything."

Tears began to run down Betty's face. "I like you so much," she sobbed. "You're so nice and friendly and kind. I wish we didn't have to go. I wish we had the chance of staying to show you we could be nice too."

"So do I," said Tommy, suddenly, and he turned very red. "I liked you all too. I was just boasting and showing off. I—I can't ride a bicycle—or a horse either. I'm not half as decent as you, Jack, nor half as brave as Benjy here."

The three Happy House children listened in surprise. They suddenly liked Tommy much better than they had ever liked him before.

"Well," said Jack, "you *must* be really brave to say all those things! I should hate to. I wish you were staying now, because we'd play with you again, and be real friends."

"Let's go and ask Miss Plum if they can stay!" said Jane. "No—*I'll* go and ask her! You wait here!" She sped away to find Miss Plum. She was in her sitting-room, doing her flowers.

"Miss Plum! Do let Tommy and Betty stay a bit longer!" cried Jane. "They're sorry for everything now. Really they are. We might teach them a lot of things now, if you'll let them stay. They'll learn now, but they wouldn't before. Can they stay?"

"Oh Jane, I hoped you'd come and ask me that!" said Miss Plum, and she kissed her. "You taught them a great lesson yesterday—you and the thunderstorm between you. Maybe you'll make them into nicer children. Yes, they can stay a little longer!"

So Tommy and Betty stayed. And this time it was Jack who was the chief and the leader and the head. It was Jack who ordered everything, and chose everything. He was always just and fair, the best leader there could possibly be.

And Tommy and Betty began to copy him and the others in all they did. They even ran errands for Miss Plum without grumbling, and they didn't chase or tease the kitten any more.

When Betty found that Jane had to make her own bed and the boys' too, she made hers and Tommy's. And she and Tommy found out how much the new glass would be to mend the cucumber frame, and took it from their purses to give Miss Plum.

"Now that really *is* nice of you, my dears!" said Miss Plum. "That really does show me you are sorry and want to do better."

"Well—it was Jane who said we ought to," said Tommy. "We didn't think of it ourselves."

Miss Plum let them take the money to pay the bill for the glass. When they came back there were five enormous ice-creams on the table.

"Go and call the others," said Miss Plum. "It's so hot I thought you would all like a treat!"

Soon Jack, Jane and Benjy were sitting in the cool sitting-room with Tommy and Betty, enjoying the lovely ice-creams. The kitten came too, but it didn't like the taste of them. Patter loved them, and everyone gave him a bit.

" I ought to have got him one too," said Miss Plum. " I forgot how much he likes them."

Tommy and Betty stayed for four days more. Then they went. " I expect you're glad to see us go! " said Tommy, as Jack, Jane and Benjy went with them to the bus.

" Oh, no! We'll look forward to your coming again! " said Jane. She noticed that this time Tommy was carrying the heavy bag, and not giving it to someone else to take. He had seen how good Jack always was to Jane, his sister, and he was copying him in that too, and trying to be good to Betty.

" Here's the bus! " said Jack. " Well, good-bye. It's been fun playing with you."

" Only the last four days," said Benjy, honestly. " I didn't like it before that. Good-bye! "

" Goodbye—and thanks for everything! " cried Tommy, from the bus.

Jack, Jane, Benjy and Patter went home. They felt quite lonely now that Tommy and Betty had gone. But Hannah was waiting for them with a nice job.

" Here you are at last! " she cried. " Which of you will pick me twelve pounds of ripe greengages from the tree at the bottom of the garden before the wasps get them all? I'm going to make jam to-day! "

Well—what a lovely job! Down the garden they rushed with baskets, and even Patter took one in his mouth!

CHAPTER SEVEN

A Visit to the Farm

ONE DAY Jack hurt his foot on a stone, and it made him limp. " It's bruised," said Mummy. " It will be all right in a day or two. You mustn't walk very much on it to-day."

" But it's the day I fetch the eggs and butter for you from the farm," said Jack.

" *I'll* go and get them," said Benjy. " I know the way now."

" No, dear, you're too little," said Mummy.

" Oh, Mummy—yesterday you said I was too big to cry because I got a thorn in my finger and to-day you say I'm too little to go to the farm," said Benjy. " Which am I, little or big? I really would like to know."

Mummy laughed. " You're mixed," she said. " But I couldn't let you go to the farm alone, Benjy dear. It's too far."

" *I'll* go with him," said Jane. " We can fetch the eggs and the butter together. I'll take Angela in her pram."

" Oh—could Monkey go too? " asked Benjy. " He would so like that. He never goes out in a pram."

" All right. You get him," said Jane. " I'll get out my pram. We'll have to go by the lane to the farm, because I can't very well take my pram over the fields."

Soon they set off. Angela was sitting up at one end of the pram, and Monkey at the other. "He does so like to see everything we pass," said Benjy. "Can I have a turn at pushing the pram, Jane—just a little turn?"

"Perhaps coming back you can," said Jane. "Angela, look at the red poppies by the wayside. Look out, Benjy, here comes a bicycle."

"I can see it," said Benjy. "You needn't tell me things like that. I'm not Angela. Do you think we shall see Amanda at the farm, Jane?"

Amanda was the farmer's little girl. Patter had come from the farm. Amanda had given him to them, and they always told Amanda all the things he had done, whenever they saw her.

"I wish Patter had come with us," said Jane. "But Jack wanted him. Anyway, he might have chased the hens, like he did last time."

They came to the farm. It was a nice farm with all kinds of noises. The ducks quacked on the pond. The hens clucked everywhere, for they ran about free. A big pig grunted loudly in a sty.

"A farm is nice and noisy and smelly," said Benjy, sniffing in delight. "I shall be a farmer when I grow up."

"You said you were going to be a bus conductor," said Jane.

"That was yesterday," said Benjy. "To-day I feel as if I'm going to be a farmer. Oh, Jane, there's Amanda. Hi, Amanda, Amanda!"

Amanda was busy. She was cleaning out the hen-house, and she had on a very old and dirty overall. She looked very happy as she poked her head out to see them.

" I'm having a lovely time," she said. " It's a bit smelly, but it's nice to be inside the hen-house. I've sat down in all the nesting boxes."

" Now don't you let Jane and Benjy get inside the hen-house! " called Amanda's mother. " They're clean, but you aren't, you little scamp. Have you come for the eggs and butter, Jane? "

" Oh, can't we just sit in *one* of the nesting boxes? " begged Benjy. " I would so like to know what it feels like to be a hen."

" No, not in that clean suit," said Amanda's mother. " If you want to sit in nesting-boxes you must come dirty and in old clothes! And don't you get in the dog's kennel either, as you did last time, Benjy. Here are the eggs and butter, Jane. Will they go in that lovely doll's pram? "

" Yes. Under the cover," said Jane. " Angela can look after them."

" No. Monkey will," said Benjy.

" They both will," said Amanda's mother, and she tucked the eggs and butter cosily under the pram-cover. " I hope they won't be too heavy for Angela's toes! "

" Amanda, come and look at my pram! " called Jane. But Amanda didn't want to. She didn't like dolls or prams or toys. She liked the dogs and the ducks, the pigs and the cows, and she would clean out any shed or house she was allowed to. Mummy said she was a proper little farmer.

Jane and Benjy set off back home. " We might pick some poppies in the lane," said Benjy. " I like their red petals and their black middles. They have soot in the middle, Jane. I got some on my nose the other day."

" Listen—what's that? " said Jane, stopping. Round the corner of the lane came the sound of boys laughing, and then of something mewing.

Jane was rather afraid of big boys. She wondered whether she would go home another way. But then she heard that mewing sound again, and she thought she would go and see what it was.

So she hurried round the corner with Benjy and the pram. She saw three boys there, bigger than Jack. In the corner by the hedge they had a little black kitten.

One of the boys was trying to hold the kitten down, and another boy was tying something to its tail. It was a tin lid on a long bit of string.

" Now, when we let the kitten go, it will run off and drag the lid behind it! " said one of the boys. " My word, it will get such a fright that it will go like lightning! "

" Mew-ew-ew—! " said the kitten, in a piteous little voice.

CHAPTER EIGHT

The Little Black Kitten

JANE FORGOT all about being afraid of big boys. She pushed the pram-handle into Benjy's hands and rushed up to the three boys.

" What are you doing? Leave that kitten alone! You bad, wicked boys! "

The boys looked at her and laughed. One of them pushed her away. " It's not *your* kitten! " said the boy. " It's a stray! Doesn't belong to anyone."

" It's *my* kitten! " suddenly said Jane, in a very loud voice. Benjy was filled with surprise. Whatever did Jane mean? It wasn't her kitten! They hadn't got a kitten. Jane was telling a story!

" 'Tisn't," said a boy.

" I tell you it *is*! " said Jane and she stamped her foot. " And I'm going straight to the policeman to tell him you're hurting my kitten! Let it go! "

The boys had finished tying the lid to the little thing's tail now. They let it go. It shot away, and the tin lid jumped after it with a clatter. The kitten was terrified.

" Mew-ew-ew! " she said, and rushed on in fear. The tin lid raced behind her, tied to her tail. The kitten was so frightened that she didn't look where she was going—and she ran straight into a little pond by the wayside. Splash! In she went. The boys laughed. Jane cried out and rushed to the little pond. She had to wade in and get the kitten, which was almost drowning.

"Now, what's going on here?" suddenly said a grown-up's voice "Bill—Harry—Walter—are you teasing that little girl?"

"They were hurting the kitten!" yelled Benjy. "They're wicked and cruel. Jane's got the kitten out of the pond. Jane, Jane, wait, I'm coming."

He hurried to Jane with the pram. The three boys were getting a fine scolding from the man, but Benjy didn't bother to stop and hear it. He wanted to get to Jane.

Jane was crying. "Oh, the poor little thing," she said. "Look, Benjy, it's trembling and shivering and it's as wet as can be. Oh, we must take it home and dry it."

"Put it into the pram," said Benjy. "I'll take Monkey and Angela out and carry them. Put it into the pram and cover it up. Oh, Jane, you *are* brave!"

"I'm not," wept Jane. "Just see how I'm crying. But I can't stop, because I'm so sorry for the kitten. How can people do those things?"

Benjy took Monkey and Angela out of the pram. He moved the butter and eggs to the end. Then Jane put the trembling kitten into the pram and covered it up. It lay quite still and good.

"Mummy will know what to do," said Benjy, trying to comfort Jane. "She always knows. Don't cry, Jane."

They wheeled the kitten home. Jane wiped her

eyes and stopped crying. Benjy trotted beside her with Monkey and Angela. It was very exciting to have a kitten in the pram, he thought.

As soon as Jane got to the gate she called Mummy and Jack. " Come here quickly," she said. " Do come! "

So they came and when Jane pulled back the cover of the pram and showed them the wet, trembling kitten, they could hardly believe their eyes.

Benjy and Jane told them all about it. Mummy gently lifted the kitten out and sat down with it in her lap. " Go and get a warm towel from the linen cupboard," she said to Jane. " And you, Benjy, ask Hannah for a little warm milk. We will soon have the kitten right."

She untied the string from its tail. When Jane brought the warm towel she gently rubbed the kitten dry. It let her do what she wanted. It knew she wouldn't hurt it or tease it.

"There!" said Mummy, and set it gently down on the ground. "It's dry. What a funny, thin little thing it is. Is that the milk, Hannah? Thank you. Now, Kitten, lap it up."

The kitten went to the milk and lapped every drop with its tiny pink tongue. The children watched it. After it had lapped it sat down and began to wash its face.

"Oh, hasn't it got good manners!" said Jane. "Washing after meals like that. Look, Benjy, it uses its paw like a sponge, wiping its face round and round."

"I wish we could keep it," said Jack. "I do so love kittens. It hasn't got a home, Mummy. I do wish we could keep it."

"Mummy—I told a dreadful story to those boys," said Jane, suddenly. "Oh, Mummy, I don't know why I did, because you know I don't tell untruths."

"Yes I heard you tell that story," said Benjy, remembering. "You gave me a surprise, Jane."

"I gave myself a surprise," said Jane, and she looked at Mummy with rather a red face. "Mummy, I wanted to stop those boys from teasing the kitten, and I told them it was *my* kitten. I knew it wasn't, but I said it was."

Mummy looked at Jane's anxious red face and she smiled. She picked up the kitten and put it into

Jane's arms. " Funny little girl! " she said. " It is your kitten! You shall have it and keep it. You thought it was a story, but it wasn't—because it is your very own kitten! You made it yours! "

" Oh, *Mummy*! " said Jane, and buried her face in the kitten's soft fur. " Thank you! It didn't belong to anyone, it was just a stray. And now it's mine. You're mine, Kitten, my very own."

" Can I have a share of it? " asked Benjy.

" Yes, you can—and Jack, too. It shall be the Happy House kitten, like Patter is the Happy House dog," said Jane, joyfully. " Oh, listen—it's purring! It *likes* belonging to us! "

CHAPTER NINE

Patter and Jumpy

"WHERE'S Patter?" said Jack. "He was here with me before you came in? We'll show him the kitten."

But Patter had gone after the butcher-boy down the road. He loved the butcher-boy. He thought he smelt nicer than anyone in the world.

"The only thing that worries me is that Patter might hurt the kitten," said Jane, looking anxious. "It would be dreadful if Patter teased it. Poor little thing, it has had enough teasing."

"Patter chases hens sometimes," said Benjy. "He might chase the kitten."

"We'll have to tie him up," said Jack.

"Oh, he'll be unhappy," said Benjy. "We'll have to keep the kitten indoors, in our playroom. We can shut the door. Then Patter won't be able to tease it."

"It's going to have a black, black coat," said Jane, and she stroked it. "Soft as silk. And it has green eyes. Listen to it purring. I wish I could purr."

"I wish I could too," said Benjy, and he tried.

"Don't do that. You're frightening the kitten," said Jane. "What shall we call it?"

"Blackie," said Benjy. "Sooty. Green-eyes. Paddy-Paws."

" Don't think of so many names at once," said Jack. " You muddle me."

" *I'm* going to choose its name," said Jane. "It's *my* kitten. But I just can't think of one at the moment."

" Oh, here's Patter," said Jack. " I'll catch him and hold him. I won't let him get near the kitten."

He caught Patter and held him. Patter scented the kitten and tried to get to it to smell it. But Jack wouldn't let him.

" You're not to frighten the kitten," he told Patter. " If you do we'll be cross with you."

They took the kitten into the playroom and shut the door. Patter whined outside. Benjy couldn't help feeling rather sad for him.

The kitten became very lively. It leapt about and chased its own tail. It jumped on to the top of the bookcase and down again. It jumped up to a chair, chased its tail there and fell off. Then it jumped on to Jane's knee and played with a button on her frock.

" You're very jumpy !" said Jane, tickling it. " A jumpy little kitten. Oh—Jack, that's what I'll call it—Jumpy! "

" That's a very *good* name for a kitten," said Jack, and Benjy nodded. " Yes, lovely. Jumpy, Jumpy, Jumpy! Do you like your name? "

The kitten lay on Jane's knee and purred. " Jumpy, you're our own kitten now," said Jane. " We've got Patter and Jumpy. What nice names they sound together—Patter and Jumpy. Patter patters about, and Jumpy jumps about! "

Patter whined outside. " I'll go and play with him," said Benjy. " I don't want him to feel left out. I know what a horrid feeling that is."

So he slipped out to play with Patter down by the stream at the end of the garden, whilst Jane and Jack played with the black kitten.

Everyone was pleased about the kitten. Mummy loved it. Daddy was amused by it too. As for Hannah, she was delighted.

" I'm sure there's a mouse in the larder," she said, " and I'll be glad to have a kitten growing up to catch it."

The children were very careful to keep Patter away from the kitten. They were so afraid he might bite it or chase it.

" If he frightens Jumpy, she might run away and never come back," said Benjy.

One day, after they had had their dinner, the children went into the playroom to find Jumpy. She wasn't there. Jane pointed to the window.

" We left the window open," she said. " Jumpy must have gone out—and, oh dear, Patter was in the garden. I do hope he hasn't bitten her! "

Mummy came in and heard. She looked out into the garden and then she laid her hand on Jane's arm. " Don't open the garden door yet," she said. " Look out there! "

The children looked out into the garden. They saw Patter lying down asleep. They saw Jumpy creeping quietly up to him, not in the least afraid!

And then Jumpy leapt right up to Patter and banged him hard on his nose with her paw! Before Patter knew what it was that had wakened him Jumpy was half-way up a tree. Patter growled and put his head down again. He shut his eyes.

Down the tree came Jumpy, very quietly. She crept up to Patter and jumped at his tail. He awoke again and leapt up. He faced round to Jumpy.

But did Jumpy run away? Not a bit of it! She sat up on her hind-legs and smacked the puppy on the nose again!

" Woof! " barked Patter, in surprise. He made as if he was going to dart at Jumpy. The kitten ran away and Patter chased her. Up a tree she went, and Patter couldn't reach her.

As soon as Patter had sat down again, the kitten

dropped on to his back. Mummy began to laugh.

"I don't think we need worry about Patter teasing Jumpy," she said. "I think it will be the other way round. Jumpy will tease poor Patter!"

"She's not a bit afraid of him," said Jane, laughing too, as she saw Jumpy trying to play with Patter's tail. "And she'll always be able to jump out of his way if he gets cross. Oh, Mummy—aren't they funny together! Can we let them always be together now, if they want to?"

"Oh yes," said Mummy, and she opened the door that led into the garden. "We needn't be afraid that Patter will worry Jumpy—we shall just have to be careful that Jumpy doesn't scare Patter!"

Patter and Jumpy both came racing across the grass as soon as they heard the playroom door open. Patter licked everyone's legs. Jumpy pounced on Mummy's shoes. They were a mad little couple!

Jumpy grew plump and her coat shone like black silk. Her eyes were still green as Miss Plum's cucumbers, and she had long white whiskers. She was the lovingest, liveliest, naughtiest kitten any family could wish for.

And very soon, at night when Patter lay down in his basket, Jumpy crept in too! She put her little black paws round his big head and slept there, warm and safe with the puppy. How Benjy loved to see them like that!

CHAPTER TEN

A Very Hot Day

THE FIRST DAYS of September were so hot that the children wore only little sun-suits and shady hats. Benjy didn't want to wear a hat, because he said it made his hair stick together.

"You'll get sun-stroke if you don't," said Jane. "You'll be sick and go pale and get the most dreadful headache you can imagine, and be in bed for days."

"How do you know?" asked Benjy.

"Because Amanda told me," said Jane. "She got sun-stroke last year when she went out in the fields all day without a hat."

After that Benjy thought he would wear a hat. He worried about Jumpy and Patter, in case they got sun-stroke too. But Mummy said animals never did.

"You go out with Hannah and help her bring back the shopping," said Mummy. "Take Patter with you. He would like that, especially as you are going to the butcher's."

So Benjy took a basket and went with Hannah and Patter. Hannah said she would go by the toy-shop and let him look in.

Jane finished her jobs, and Jack came back from the farm with the eggs and butter he had been to fetch. His foot was quite better now. Miss Plum looked over the wall.

"I wish I was like you and could wear only a sun-suit," she said. "Why don't you bathe in your stream? It's lovely and clean, you know."

"Oh, what a good idea!" said Jane, and ran to ask Mummy. Mummy said yes, she didn't see why they shouldn't, but they mustn't put their heads under the water in case it wasn't good to swallow.

Soon Jane and Jack were sitting down in the stream. They splashed one another. It was fun. Jumpy came and watched them but she wouldn't go near the water since she had jumped into the pond when the bad boys had teased her.

"I think I'll undress Angela and put a sun-suit on her," said Jane. "She'd like that. Oh—and do you think Monkey would like a bathe, too, Jack?"

"Yes. But you'd better wait till Benjy comes back," said Jack, picking up a pebble with his toes. "Look, Jane, I can pick up stones with my toes."

But Jane had gone indoors to fetch Angela. The doll was in the playroom, sitting up in her cot. Monkey was there too, sitting on the window-sill, looking out of the window. Benjy always said Monkey liked to look out of the window.

Jane undressed Angela quickly. She had a little knitted suit for her to wear, that looked very like Jane's own sun-suit.

"There!" said Jane. "You look sweet—and soon you will feel nice and cool, Angela."

She stopped by Monkey. Surely he would like to bathe too? Well, perhaps not *really* bathe, but just wear a sun-suit and sit and watch her and Jack and Angela?

She found an old red vest belonging to a doll and put it on Monkey. Then she carried him and Angela out to the stream.

Angela had a strong rubber body and was a doll you could bath. So she was quite all right to put into the water. Jane sat her down carefully.

"It feels a tiny bit cold at first," she told her. "But it soon feels lovely. Oh, Angela, you look sweet!"

Jack splashed Angela. "She doesn't mind!" said Jane. "She's brave. Look, I've brought Monkey too. Doesn't he look funny in this old red vest!"

Jack didn't bother about Monkey and he soon got tired of Angela. He lay down in the water.

"Don't let it get into your mouth, Mummy said," said Jane. "Oh, Jack, there's a fish!"

That made Jack sit up. He and Jane sat quite quiet to make the water still again. They were in a kind of little pool with the stream flowing beyond them.

"I can see the fish again," said Jane, in a whisper. "I'll reach back and get a twig of something, Jack, and point him out to you."

She reached behind her without looking—and, oh dear, her arm bumped against Monkey, who was sitting on a nearby stone—and he lost his balance and fell right into the water.

CHAPTER ELEVEN

Benjy Loses his Temper and Finds it Again

"GOODNESS! There goes Monkey!" cried Jane, and tried to fish him out. He was very, very wet.

"Well, he's soaked now, so you might as well let him finish his bathe," said Jack, lazily. Jane sat him down in the water again and laughed.

"He looks sort of surprised," she said. "Won't Benjy laugh when he sees him!"

But Benjy didn't laugh. He came running down to the stream with Patter, ready to tell about the things in the toyshop—and he suddenly saw Monkey in the water!

Monkey had fallen on his face, and was lying like that in the stream, his long arms waving about in the water.

Benjy gave such a squeal that Jane and Jack jumped.

"Oh! Look at *Monkey*! Who put him there? He's drowning, he's drowning."

"He's not," said Jane, and she sat Monkey up. He fell forward again and dabbled his face in the water. Benjy jumped into the stream with a splash almost on top of Angela.

"You bad girl!" Benjy shouted to Jane. "How

dare you take *my* Monkey out and put a red vest on him, and drown him in the water? I'll smack you till you cry!"

And, to Jane's enormous surprise, the little boy fell on her and began to slap her as hard as he could. Slap, slap, slap! Benjy went quite mad, and, as Jane was sitting down in the water, it was difficult for her to stop him.

In the middle of all this, just as Jack was getting up to stop Benjy, Mummy came. When she saw what Benjy was doing, she was very angry.

"Benjy! Stop it at once! I will not have this behaviour. Go indoors at once."

Benjy stopped. He faced his mother, red in the face and panting. "She's a bad girl!" he sobbed. "Do you know what she did? She . . ."

"I don't want to hear anything," said Mummy. "What you did is quite enough. Go indoors and go up to bed."

"But it isn't fair!" cried Benjy, and he stamped his foot in the water and splashed everyone. "I want to tell . . ."

"GO INDOORS AT ONCE!" said Mummy and her voice sounded so stern that Benjy was shocked. He came out of the water. The tears poured down his cheeks.

"I shall never like Jane again!" he shouted. "Never! I shall never like anyone again! I shall go indoors and I shall go to bed, but I shan't ever speak to any of you again!"

He tore up the garden, went into the playroom, slammed the door and went up the stairs, leaving

little drips of water as he went. He was very angry and very hurt and very miserable. He suddenly remembered Monkey. Why, he had left him in the stream. Oh, would that horrid Jane take him out?

He looked out of the window. He saw Mummy coming up the garden. She had Monkey. She was squeezing the water out of him. Poor, poor Monkey. He must hate that. Perhaps Mummy would bring Monkey up to him.

But she didn't. She didn't come near him. She was angry, and she wasn't often angry, Benjy knew.

He suddenly felt tired. He threw off his sun-suit and got into bed. He lay down under a sheet, and sighed heavily. " I shall never be happy again," said Benjy, out loud. " Never. I wish I didn't belong to this family. It's a horrid family. I don't like any of them. I shall run away and then they'll be very, very sorry."

A tear rolled down his cheek again. "They'll never hear of me again after I've run away. I shan't let them know what happens to me. I'll leave them all, horrid unkind things!"

Benjy fell asleep. He awoke when Hannah came into the room with some dinner on a tray.

"Your mother says you must stay up here till you feel sorry for slapping Jane, and then you can come down and say so," said Hannah. "Really, Benjy, I'm surprised at you!"

"I don't like you either," said Benjy. "And I shan't eat any dinner. You can take it away. You're a horrid person too."

But Hannah didn't take the dinner away and he did eat it after all. Then, because it was so very hot, he fell asleep again.

Hannah came in with a tray of tea. It was quite a nice tea. "Now why don't you be a good boy and let me brush your hair for you, and take you downstairs to tea?" she said.

"Where's Monkey?" asked Benjy.

"He's hanging on the line to dry," said Hannah. "You can see him if you look."

Benjy was off the bed in a trice. He looked out of the window and, oh dear, there was poor, poor Monkey hanging by his tail to dry!

"What a cruel thing to do to him!" said Benjy, upset. "He's upside down—and pegged by his tail too. He must be feeling dreadful. Go and get him, Hannah."

" Not if you talk like that! " said Hannah, in a huff, and went out. Benjy ate his tea, and sulked, and wanted Monkey.

Suddenly the door opened and Jane peeped in the room. " Oh, Benjy," she said. " Oh, Benjy, they've pegged Monkey on the line. I've just seen him. He's so miserable."

" Jane, Jane! Get him for me! " begged Benjy. " Please, please do! Oh, Jane, I can't bear to see him there either. It wasn't his fault he got wet."

" No. It was mine," said Jane. " But it was an accident. He fell in."

" Oh," said Benjy. " Well, please, Jane, go and get Monkey for me."

Jane went out of the room. She ran down the stairs and into the garden. There was no one there. Benjy watched her unpeg Monkey quickly. He hugged himself for joy.

" Dear Jane! " he said. " Dear kind Jane! Now I shall soon have Monkey! "

Jane came in with Monkey. He still felt rather damp. Jane sat on the bed with Benjy, and they tried to warm Monkey together.

" Thank you, Jane, oh thank you! " said Benjy. " You're the kindest girl! "

Then he remembered how he had slapped Jane, and he looked at her. " Jane! I'm sorry I slapped you. It was only because I thought you were drowning Monkey."

" As if I *would*! " said Jane. " I love Monkey as much as you do. He used to go to bed with *me* before you had him. I tell you, he fell in. I put him on a stone to watch me and Jack and Angela. He was waiting for you."

"I didn't know that," said Benjy, and he looked sad and ashamed. "I lost my temper and I hit you, and I know I should never hit a girl. Are you very angry, Jane?"

"No, not now," said Jane. "I know how you must have felt when you thought I was drowning Monkey—like *I* felt when I saw those boys teasing poor Jumpy. It's all right, Benjy. I love you again."

"And I love my family again," said Benjy, happily. "I shan't run away after all. I nearly did, Jane."

"You always say that," said Jane. "Come on downstairs and have some plums. We've been picking them."

So Benjy went downstairs with Jane. "I've said I'm sorry," he said to Mummy. "And I am. I won't do it again."

"Well, come and sit by me and I'll find you a ripe plum," said Mummy. "Is Monkey dry yet? Almost. Sit him in the sunshine again, but don't give him any plum or he'll get sticky."

It was nice sitting there in the sun. Mummy was sewing. Jack was making paper-boats. Jane was playing with Jumpy and Patter. Hannah was humming in the kitchen.

"I couldn't possibly run away from this nice family," said Benjy to Mummy. "I've been silly and bad. I'll be extra good now and make up for it. Jane was so nice to go and fetch Monkey for me."

Miss Plum looked over the wall. " What a nice happy family you all look, sitting together in the evening sun! " she called.

" Yes," called back Mummy. " Even Benjy thinks he won't run away from us all! *Isn't* that a good thing? "

And how everybody laughed—Benjy too!

CHAPTER TWELVE

A Picnic on Breezy Hill

"WE'LL go for a picnic, I think," said Daddy one Saturday. "We'll go in the car to Breezy Hill, and feel the wind on our faces. Can you pack us up a nice lunch, Mummy?"

The children were pleased. They all loved a picnic. "You shall come too, Patter," said Jane.

"And Jumpy as well?" asked Benjy. "Jumpy doesn't like to be left out."

"No, not Jumpy," said Mummy. "You can't take cats on a picnic."

"What a pity!" said Benjy. "Jumpy will be lonely. Is Hannah coming too?"

"Yes, we'll take Hannah as well," said Mummy. "She will love it. I'll go and get the picnic hamper ready."

The picnic hamper was almost as big as the laundry basket! It had belonged to Daddy's family, and as they had been a big family and had often gone for picnics, they had had to have an enormous hamper.

Now Daddy had the hamper for his own little family. It took pork pies and ham, tarts and sandwiches, apples and ginger-beer quite easily.

"We can stuff the corners with paper," said Mummy. She and Hannah cut sandwiches quickly. Patter and Jumpy came to watch them. Patter was excited. He liked the smell of pork-pies and he liked to know they were all going for a picnic. Perhaps he could chase a rabbit!

Jumpy sat on the window-sill and watched everything. She jumped down and tried to jump on to the table but Hannah sent her down. She wasn't allowed on any table at all.

"*Can't* Jumpy come with us?" begged Benjy. "Just this once? She does so want to. She'll feel dreadful left behind without even Hannah or Patter here."

"She'll curl up in the sun and sleep all the time," said Hannah.

"She won't. Look how wide awake she is!" said Benjy.

"Now you go away and don't come bothering me," said Hannah. "And take your fingers out of that meat paste. Ah, it's no wonder the kitten comes to you and you all over potted meat!"

"Mummy, can we shut Jumpy up in the playroom, with Patter's basket to sleep in, and her ball to play with?" asked Benjy. "Just so she won't feel too bad?"

"Yes, we'll do that," said Mummy. "Now go away before you upset the milk."

At last everything was ready. Daddy had got the car out. The hamper was put in the back of it. Patter was sitting on the back seat with Jack. Hannah was putting on her hat. Mummy was locking the back door.

"Mummy—I can't find Jumpy," said Benjy, appearing in the kitchen, looking worried.

" Well, she's somewhere about," said Mummy. " I shooed her down from the table again, the last time I saw her."

" Well, I want to put her in the playroom, with Patter's basket and her ball," said Benjy. " I've got them all ready."

" Oh dear, Benjy, don't begin worrying about Jumpy! " said Mummy. " She can look after herself now! "

" She can't," said Benjy. " Just suppose we left her out-of-doors, Mummy—it might rain—or a strange dog might come in and chase her—or someone might come and steal her."

" Well, you've got two minutes to look for her, and then, if you haven't found her, you must leave her and get in the car," said Mummy. " Or else you will be left behind."

Poor Benjy! He couldn't find Jumpy anywhere and he really was very nearly left behind. He heard Daddy starting up the car, and just ran down the path in time.

" I do think you're unkind to leave poor Jumpy like this," he said. " I feel upset about her."

" I do a bit too," Jane said to him. " I hope that big dog down the road doesn't come in and get her."

This was a most alarming thought. Benjy's face grew very long indeed.

" I shan't enjoy the picnic now," he thought. " I shan't want any of those lovely tarts to eat! "

It was lovely up on Breezy Hill. Benjy forgot about Jumpy as he tore up and down. But he remembered again when they all sat down to their lunch, and Daddy put the picnic basket down in the middle of them.

"I've remembered Jumpy," said Benjy, sadly. "I thought I heard a mew just then, and it reminded me."

"I thought I heard a mew too," said Jane. Mummy laughed. "What dreadful children you are! I expect at this very moment, Jumpy is having a lovely game with Miss Plum's kitten next door," she said.

And then *everyone* heard a *mew*! It was most extraordinary. Mummy looked all round but she couldn't see a cat.

"Do you think it's Jumpy in trouble at home and calling for help?" said Jane.

"Don't be silly, Jane," said Mummy, and opened the hamper. She had stuffed the empty corners with papers, as she had said she would. She pulled them out—and my goodness, what was this coming out with the paper?

Yes—it was Jumpy! "Mew-ew-ew!" she said, in a pleased little voice. Benjy gave a yell of joy.

"She came after all! She got into the hamper so that she could come! Isn't she clever? Oh, Jumpy, I *knew* I heard you mew!"

"Mew-ew-ew! Mew-ew-ew!" said Jumpy, rubbing herself against Benjy's knee.

"She says, 'I meant to come with you-oo-oo,'" explained Benjy, and everyone laughed.

"So we've got the whole of Happy House folk after all!" said Mummy, dealing out sandwiches. "Me—and Daddy—and Hannah—and Jack—

and Jane—and Benjy—and Patter—and Jumpy too!"

"Now I'm happy, and so is Jane," said Benjy, giving Jumpy some of his meat-paste sandwich. "There's only one thing I like better than leaving Happy House and going for a picnic."

"What's that?" asked Mummy.

"Why, leaving the picnic and going back to dear old Happy House, of course!" said Benjy. "I should have thought you could have guessed *that*, Mummy!"

"Perhaps I did!" said Mummy, and she smiled her nicest smile. "Yes—I really think I did!"

THE END